The Beginner's Bible

SUPER-DUPER MIGHTY JUMBO

ACTIVITY BOOK

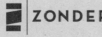

ZONDERkidz

ZONDERKIDZ

The Beginner's Bible® Super-Duper, Mighty Jumbo Activity Book
Copyright © 2012 by Zondervan
Illustrations © 2012 by Zondervan

Requests for information should be addressed to:

Zonderkidz, 3900 *Sparks Drive SE, Grand Rapids, Michigan* 49546

ISBN: 978-0-310-72499-5

Scriptures taken from the Holy Bible, *New International Reader's Version®, NIrV®.* Copyright© 1995, 1996, 1998 by Biblica, Inc.™ Used by permission of Zondervan. All rights reserved worldwide.

Illustrator: Denis Alonso
Editor: Mary Hassinger
Art direction and cover design: Cindy Davis
Interior design: Sarah Molegraaf

Printed in the United States

22 23 24 25 26 /PHP/ 15 14 13 12 11 10

God's Creation

Match It Up

God created all things in seven days. Draw a line from the number to the group that was created that day.

Connect It

Searching

Find and circle the words in the puzzle below.

BIRD   FISH   OCEAN

SKY   WATER

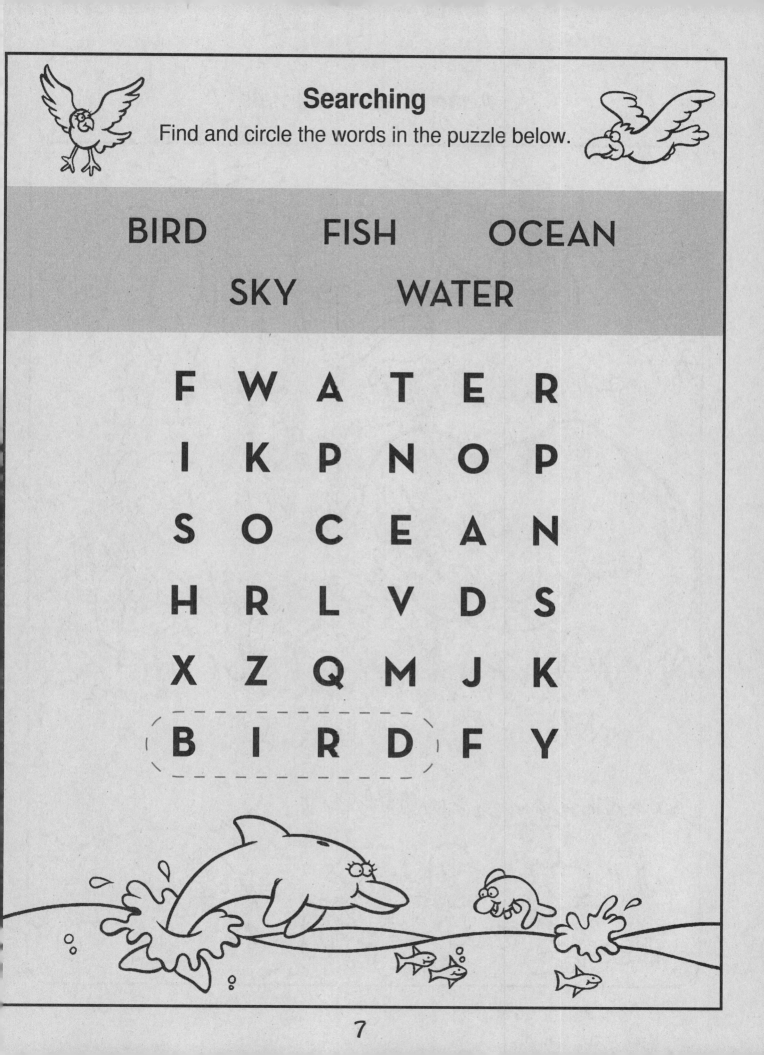

```
F  W  A  T  E  R
I  K  P  N  O  P
S  O  C  E  A  N
H  R  L  V  D  S
X  Z  Q  M  J  K
B  I  R  D  F  Y
```

Count It Out

How many are on the page? Circle the number.

1	**2**	**3**
1	2	3
3	4	5
3	4	5

Where Is Eve?

Help Adam find Eve.

God's Beauty

Which Is Bigger?

The first bird is bigger than the second one.
Circle the picture that is bigger than the first one.

Which Is Smaller?

The first fish is smaller than the second one.
Circle the picture that is smaller than the first one.

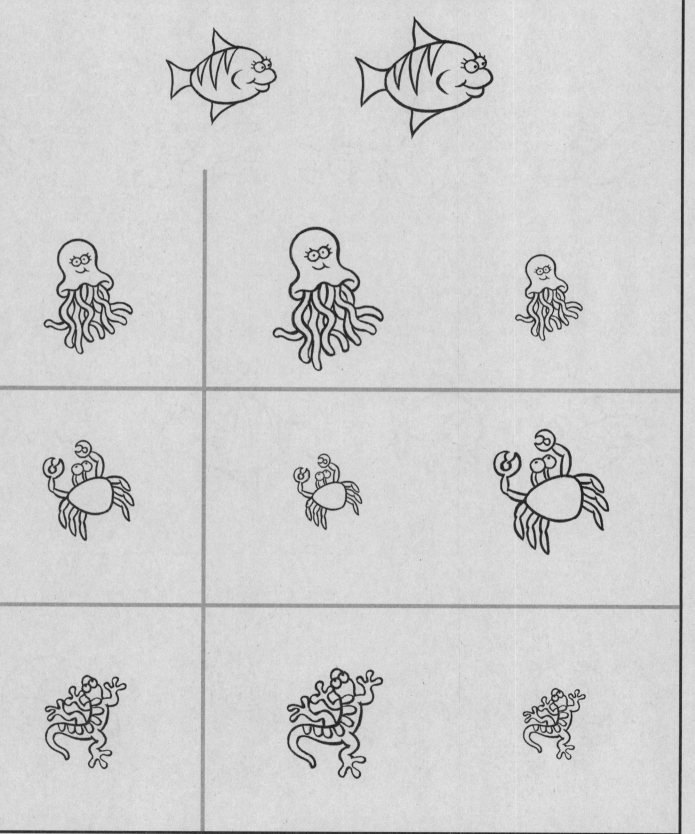

The Same

Circle two that are the same in each row.

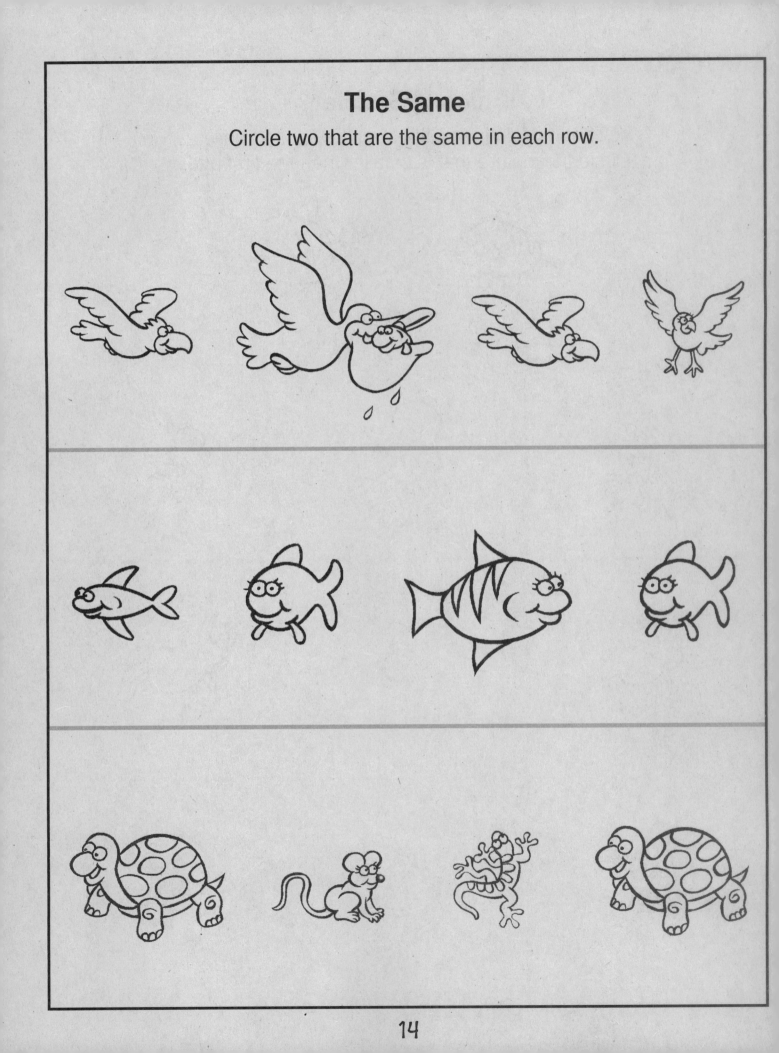

Trace the Numbers

Adam named the animals one by one. Trace the numbers.

God's Love

God loved Adam and Eve. God loves you.
Connect the dots. Color the picture.

The Garden Search

Find and circle the words in the puzzle below.

APPLE   GARDEN   LEAF

TREE   TRUNK

```
T  A  T  R  E  E  E
R  P  Q  Z  U  B
U  P  L  E  A  F
N  L  V  H  K  S
K  E  Y  J  O  X
   G  A  R  D  E  N
```

Matching

Circle the two that are exactly the same.

Which Is Which?

Circle the fish, put an X on the birds.

Animal Buddies

Match the animal pairs.

Are They the Same?

Help Eve tell the difference.
Circle the picture that is different in each row.

Adam's Apples

Adam also ate an apple from the tree.
Circle the pairs of two.

Color the Garden

God made a beautiful garden for Adam and Eve. Color the apples red.
Color the leaves and grass green. Color the trunks brown. Use your
favorite colors to color the flowers.

Where Are They?

Adam and Eve tried to hide. Draw a rectangle around them.
Color the rectangle orange.

Up-to-Down

God said the snake would crawl on its belly.
Trace the long snake.

Angels Help God

God placed angels at the entrance of the garden.
Draw a line from the angels to their matching shadows.

Noah Loved God

Noah loved God. Circle the picture that completes the pattern.

Get to Work!

God gave Noah a job to do. Draw a line to connect the pictures that belong together.

Noah's Ark

Noah built an ark which took work and practice.
Practice tracing the lines below.

Practice tracing lines top to bottom.

Practice tracing lines left to right.

Practice tracing circles.

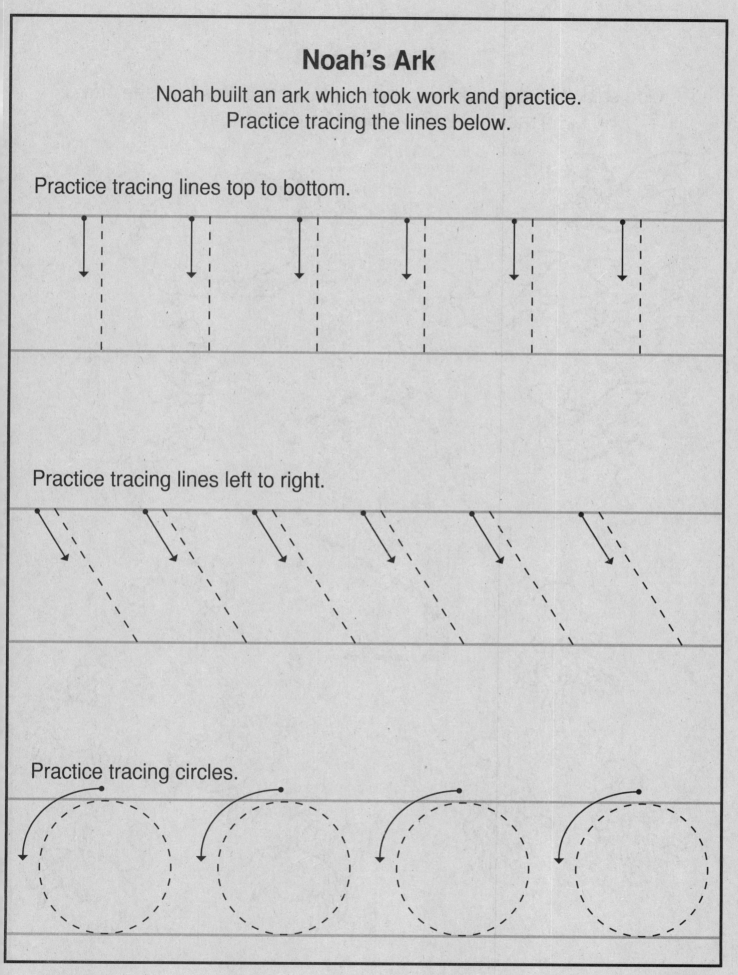

Noah Does It

God said, "Take your family and two of every animal into the ark."
Trace the 2. Color two of each creature.

How Much More?

More and more rain fell. Circle the picture with more.

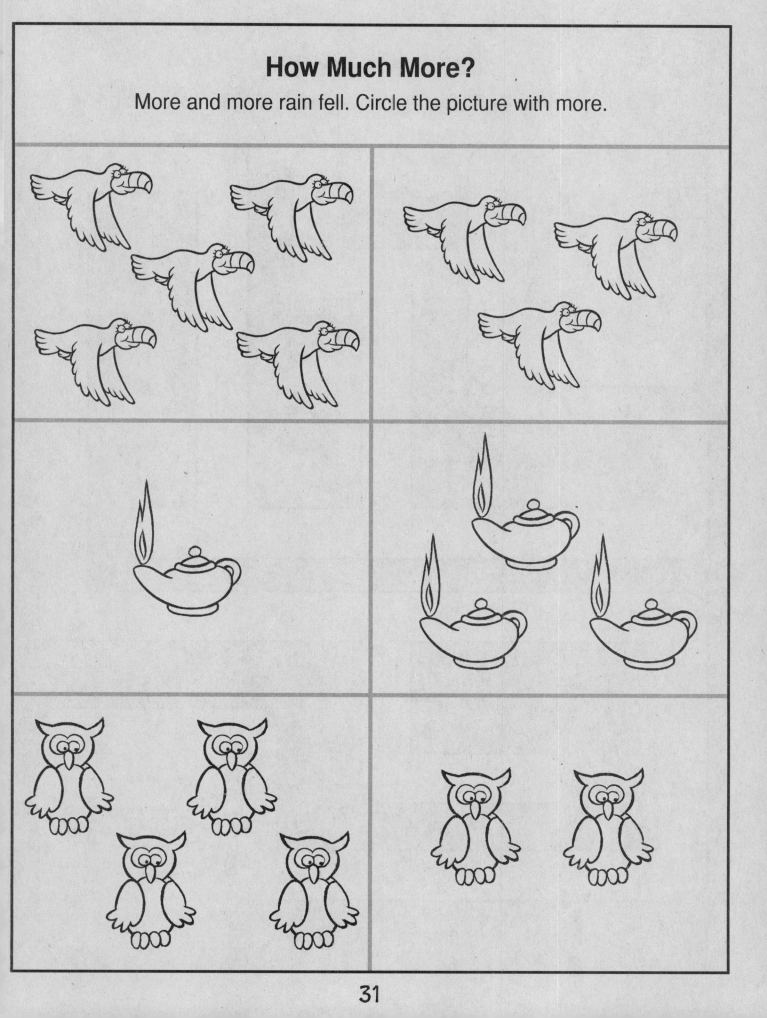

Where Is Land?

The dove found land. Help the dove find its way back to the ark.

Rainbow Bright

God put a beautiful rainbow in the sky.

Tallest

The people said, "Let's build a tall tower." Circle the picture that is taller than the first one.

All Mixed Up

God mixed up their language. Circle the pictures that are upside-down.

The Tower of Babel

Connect the dots.

Abraham Listens

God told Abraham to move to a new land. Find the path
to Abraham and Sarah's new home.

Trace the Star

God gave Abraham many blessings. Trace a star. Draw stars to fill the sky.

Visitors Come

Abraham had three visitors. Design and color a robe for each visitor.

Good Job, Sarah

Sarah made a tasty meal. Draw lines to put the things Sarah needs on the rug.

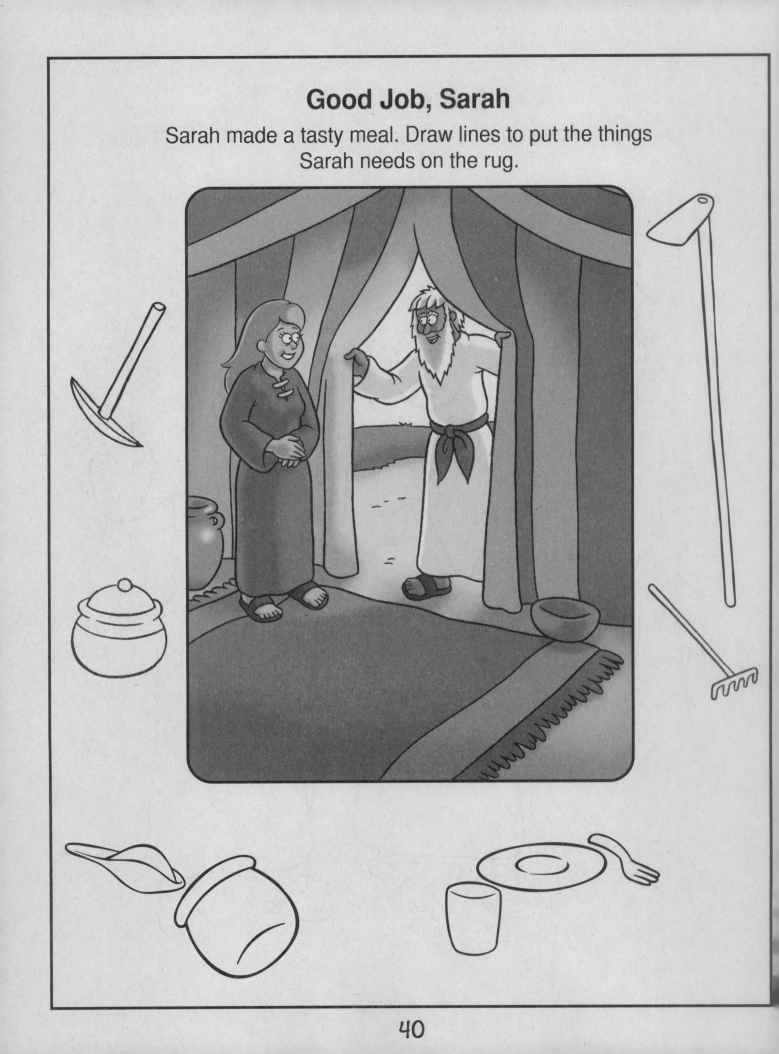

"Haha," Said Sarah

Sarah laughed. Check () the happy faces.

A Baby Boy

Sarah had a baby boy. Draw a present inside the box for the baby.

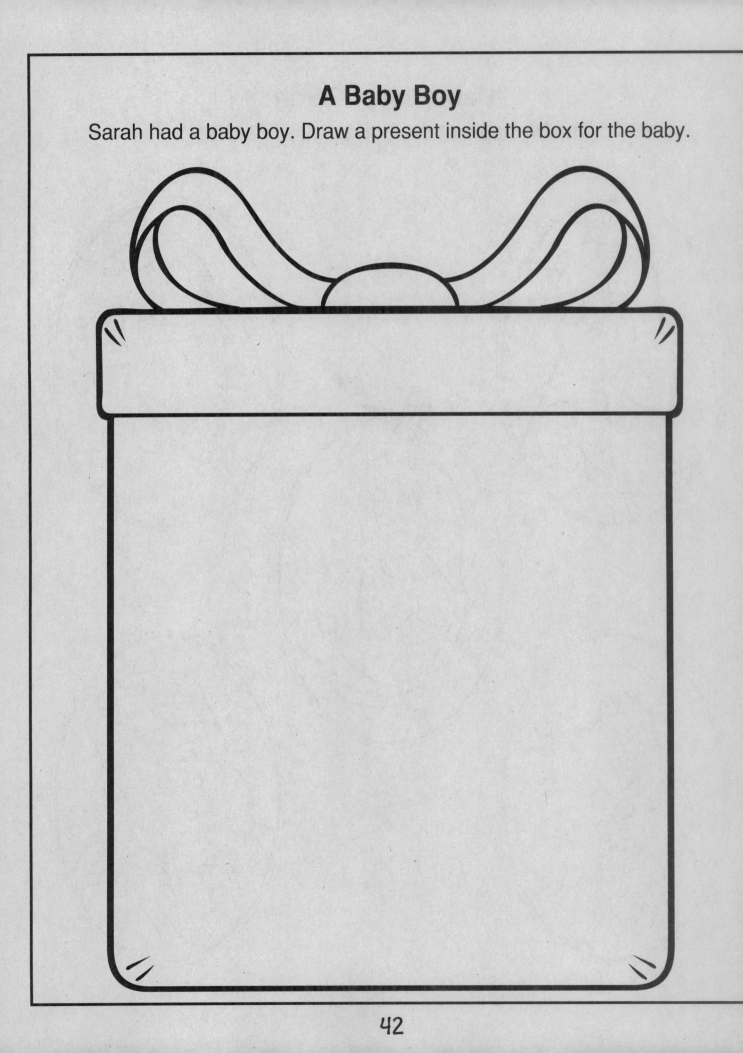

Rebekah Meets Isaac

Rebekah came to the well. Trace the circles.

43

A Wedding

God loved Isaac and Rebekah. God loves you.
Connect the dots and color the picture.

44

It Is Twins!

Jacob and Rebekah had twin sons. Circle the twins.

Isaac's Blessing

Isaac gave Jacob his blessing.
Write 1 under what happened first. Write 2 under what happened next.
Write 3 under what happened last.

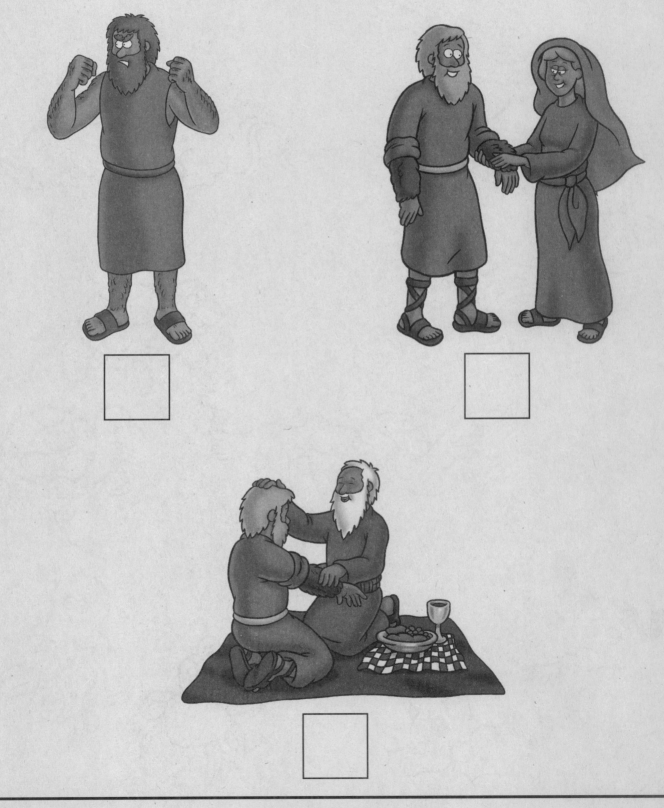

Jacob's Ladder

Jacob dreamed of angels walking up and down.
Write X on the angels going up. Circle the angels going down.

47

I Am Sorry

Jacob brought gifts to say he was sorry. What did Jacob bring?
Draw what is inside the box Jacob sent to Esau.

Who Is It?

Esau gave Jacob a hug. Read the clues.
Draw a line from the brother to his name.

1. Esau has lots of hair on his arms.
2. Jacob has straps on his sandals.

Jacob   **Esau**

Twelve Sons

Joseph was one of Jacob's 12 sons. Count the brothers. Trace the numbers.

1 2 3 4 5 6
7 8 9 10 11 12

Coat of Many Colors

Joseph had a colorful robe. Color Joseph's robe.

Poor Joseph

Joseph is far from his brothers. Draw a rope from a brother to Joseph.

Near Him

God was near Joseph. Circle the plants near Joseph.

Pharaoh's Dreams

Pharaoh had strange dreams. Draw two pictures from your dreams.

Joseph Helps

Joseph is wise. Find and circle the words in the puzzle below.

G	C	A	N	P	E	S	S	S
B	L	R	U	G	R	K	O
V	O	S	F	I	O	I	I
C	O	W	S	D	M	N	W
N	N	S	R	E	F	N	F
P	I	E	W	W	L	Y	B
X	A	P	R	R	E	V	D
M	L	I	A	J	I	M	L

A Big Job

Joseph gathered extra food. Draw one more to make extra.

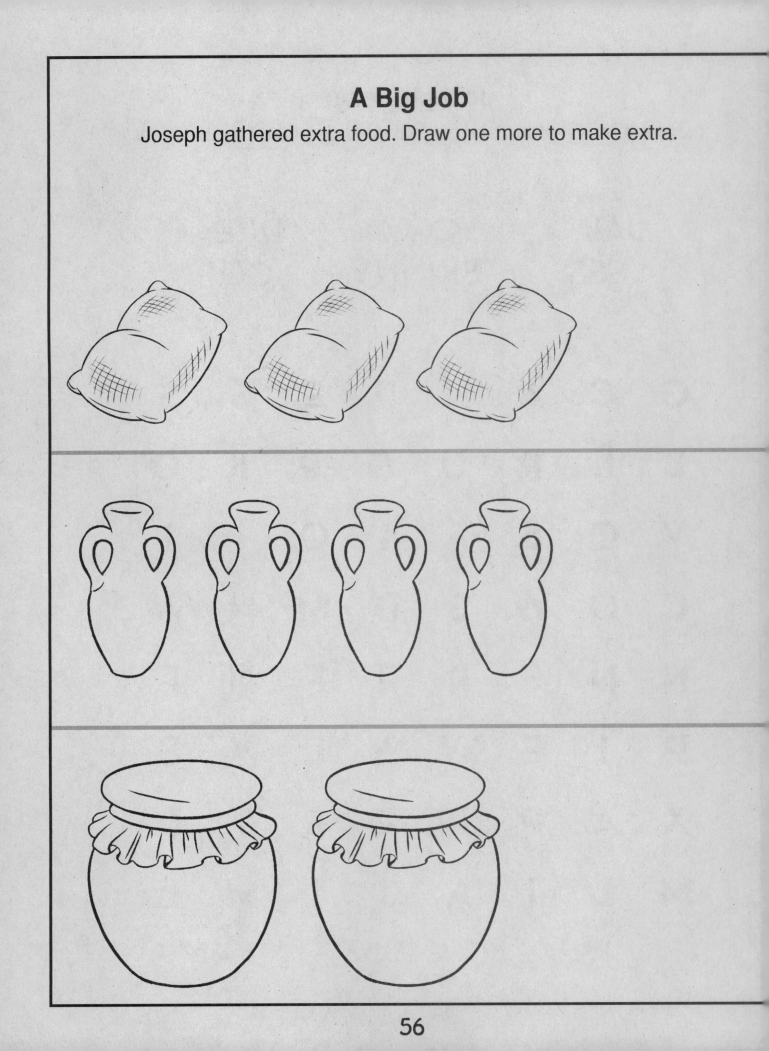

Poor Brothers

Joseph's brothers had no food. Circle what you can taste.

Save Moses

Miriam was afraid. She put Moses in a basket.
Trace ovals. Trace a basket. Draw baby Moses inside.

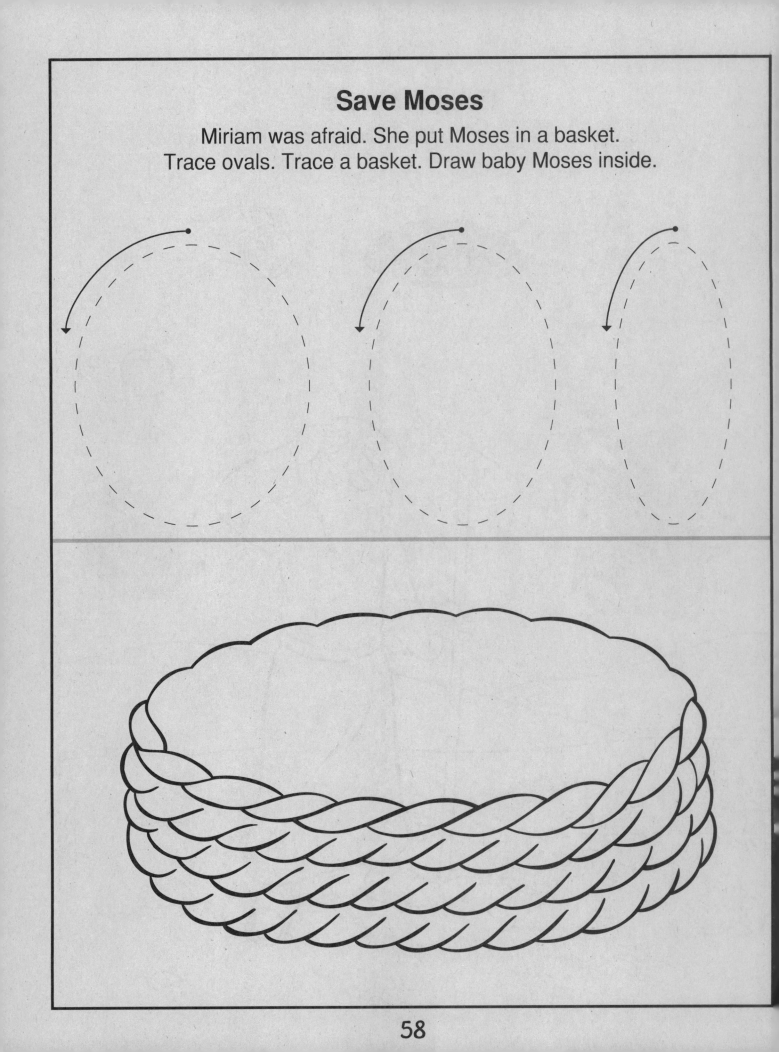

Moses Grows

Moses grew up in the palace.
Circle the picture that shows why that happened.

Counting Sheep

Moses left the palace. He became a shepherd.
Count the number of sheep with Moses. Trace that number.

On Fire

Moses saw a burning bush.
Use red, yellow, and orange crayons to draw the flames.

Moses Listens to God

Moses heard a voice in the bush. God said, "Take my people to a new land."
Circle all of the ears used to hear. Where are the snake's ears?

NO!

Pharaoh said, "NO!" Trace N. Trace O. Trace and write NO.

Count to Ten

God sent ten plagues. Trace 10. Circle groups of ten.

10 10 10 10 10

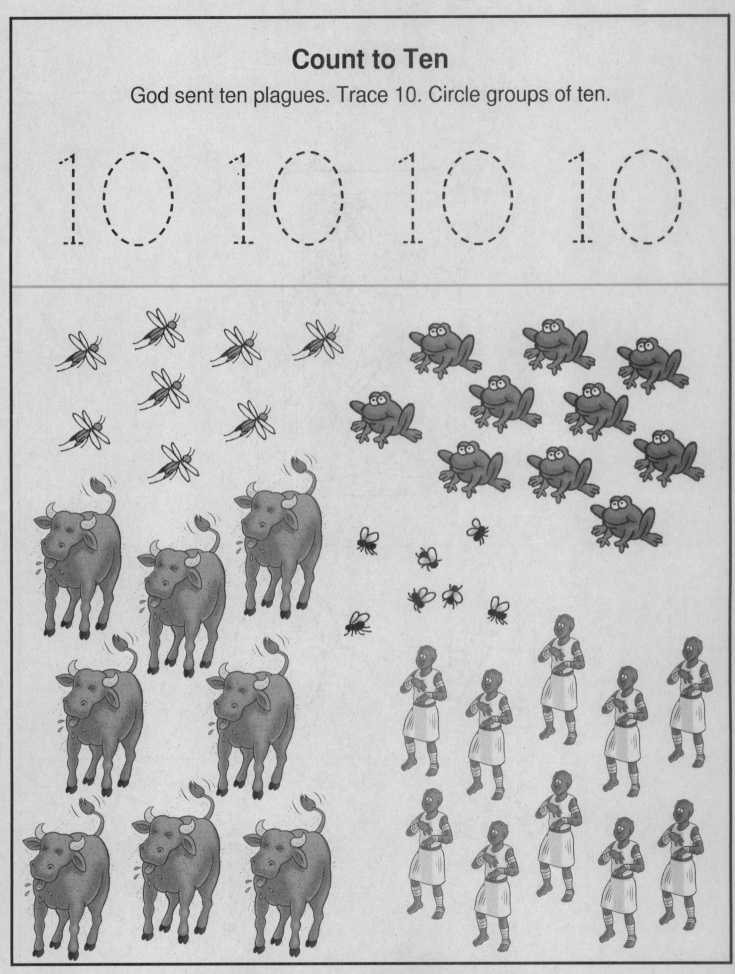

A Red River

God turned the river to blood. Color the river red.

A Little Jumpy

God sent frogs. Circle four groups of four frogs.

GO!

Finally, Pharaoh said, "GO!" Color the pictures that rhyme with GO.

GO!

PIG

FOE

CAKE

DOUGH

Where Is God?

God went ahead in cloud and fire. Circle what hid God.

Close and Far

Pharaoh was close. Make an X on what is close. Circle what is far.

Waves Apart

The Lord pushed back the sea to make a path. Trace the waves left to right.

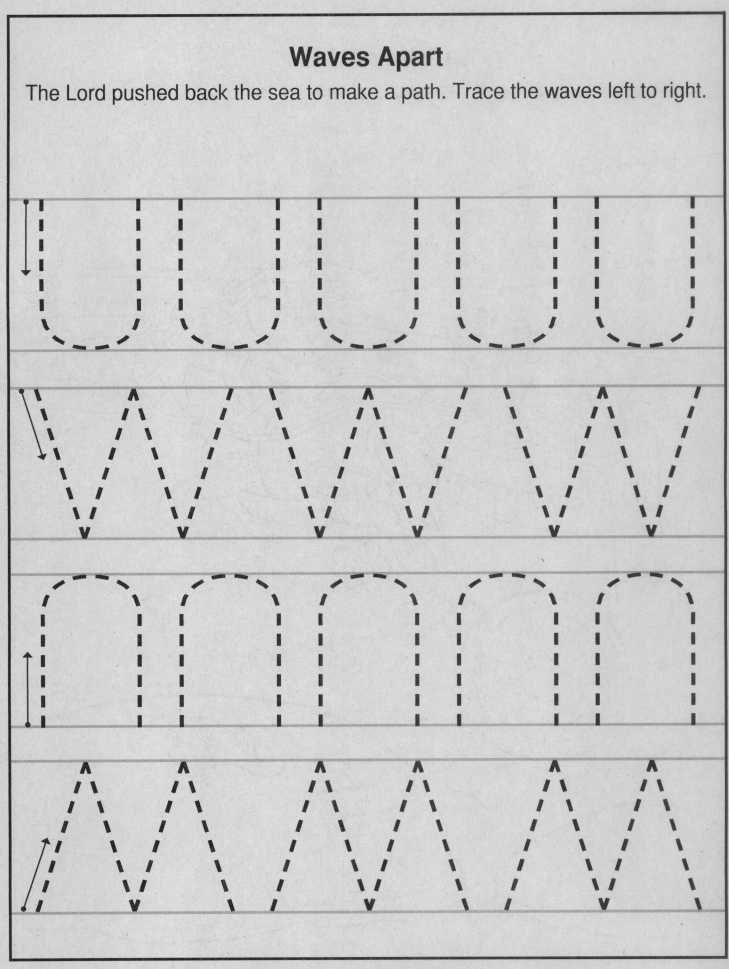

Listen for S

The people were free. They sang praises to God!
Circle the two pictures that begin with the S sound.

sandal

crab

sea

sing

donkey

X Marks the Spot

The Israelites traveled in the desert. Place an X on the pictures of the desert.

Food from God

God sent bread from heaven. It tasted like honey.
Trace six sides to make hexagons in the honeycomb.
Draw a honeybee.

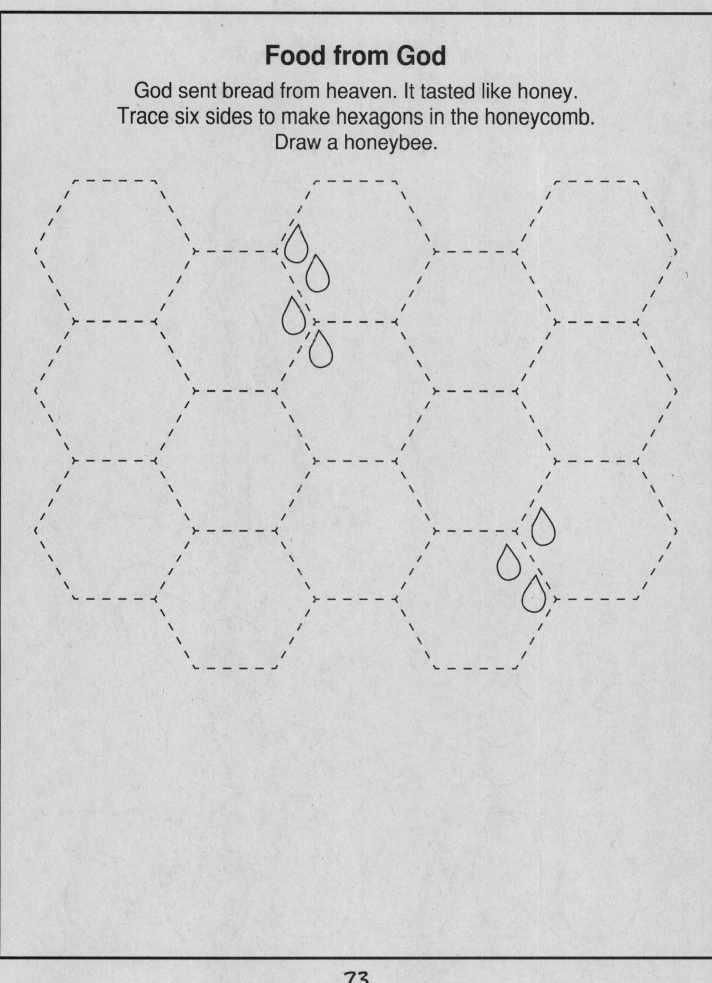

Where Is the Water?

The people were thirsty. God sent water.
Use a blue crayon to fill the containers with water.

Light the Way

God sent the Ten Commandments. Trace the paths of the lightning bolts.

Ten Rules

God wrote the Ten Commandments for the people to obey.
Trace the numbers. Count backwards from ten.

Tablet Teachings

The Ten Commandments teach the people how to behave.
Draw a picture on each tablet that shows a way
God wants his people to behave.

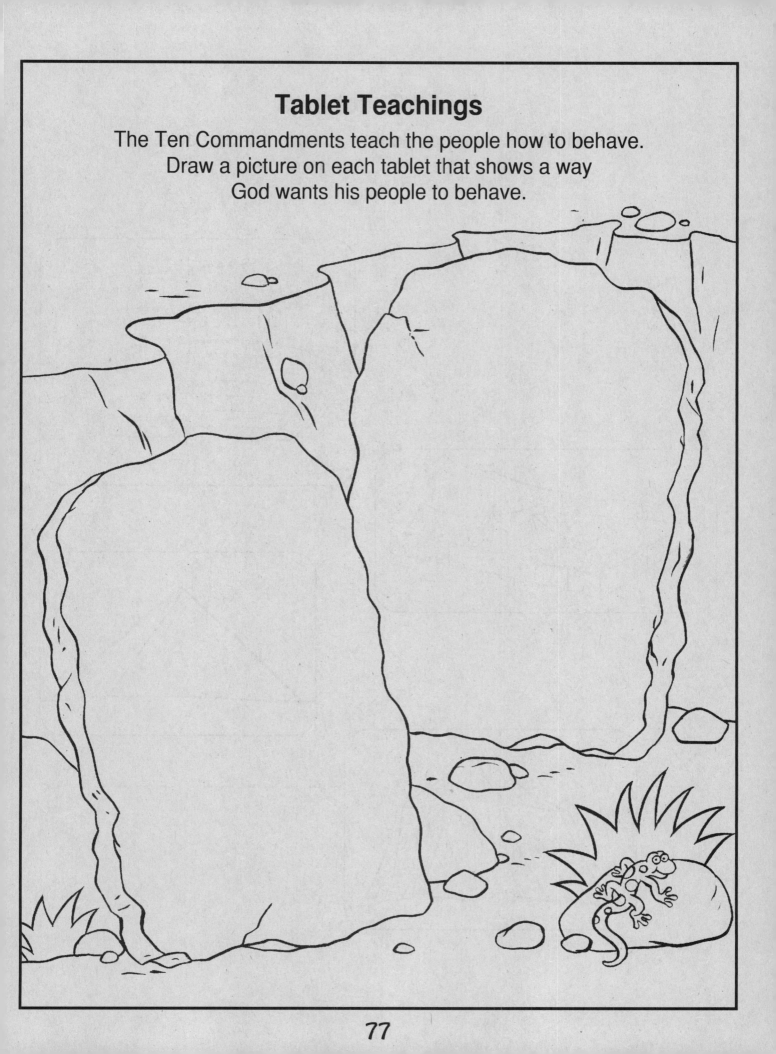

Tablet Teachings

God showed the people how to build a tabernacle.
Make an X on the tabernacle.

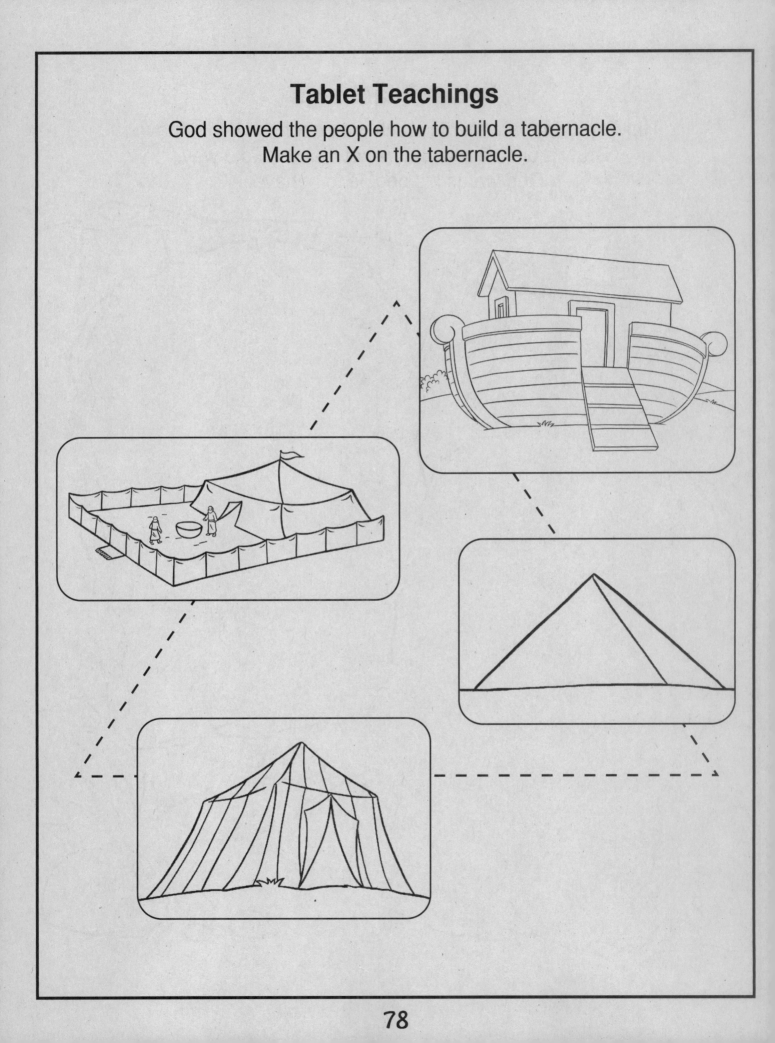

Promised Land

Finally, the people could see the Promised Land. Color the Promised Land.

Promised Land Pathway

God said the people were still not ready. Find the Promised Land.

High Up

Jericho had high walls. Circle what is high in each picture.

Rahab Helps

Rahab hid the men on her roof. Trace the shapes.
Use the shapes to draw a house. Color the roof.

Rahab's Rope

Rahab helped the men escape. Draw a rope to show how she helped.

Six Is It

God said to march for six days. Trace 6. Write 6. Circle six people.

Up and Down

The walls came tumbling down! Make a down arrow (↓) on what is down.
Make an up arrow (↑) on what is up.

Where Are the Words?

Deborah listened to God. Find and circle the words in the puzzle below.

FORGOT	GOD	PLAN
WON	GO	LEAD

```
K  C  J  L  N  M  D  O
X  J  B  J  B  A  L  L
N  D  C  B  F  P  L  Y
U  J  J  M  A  L  D  P
T  O  G  R  O  F  A  A
X  Z  H  P  D  D  E  Q
W  O  N  O  N  L  L  F
S  Q  G  J  W  V  G  Y
```

Flags

The Israelites carried flags to battle.
Use triangles to design and color flags. Add a carrying pole.

A Sign for Gideon

Gideon asked God to give him a sign. Circle what is wet.
Put an X on what is dry.

Less Than

"That is too many," God said. Circle the group that is less than the first one.

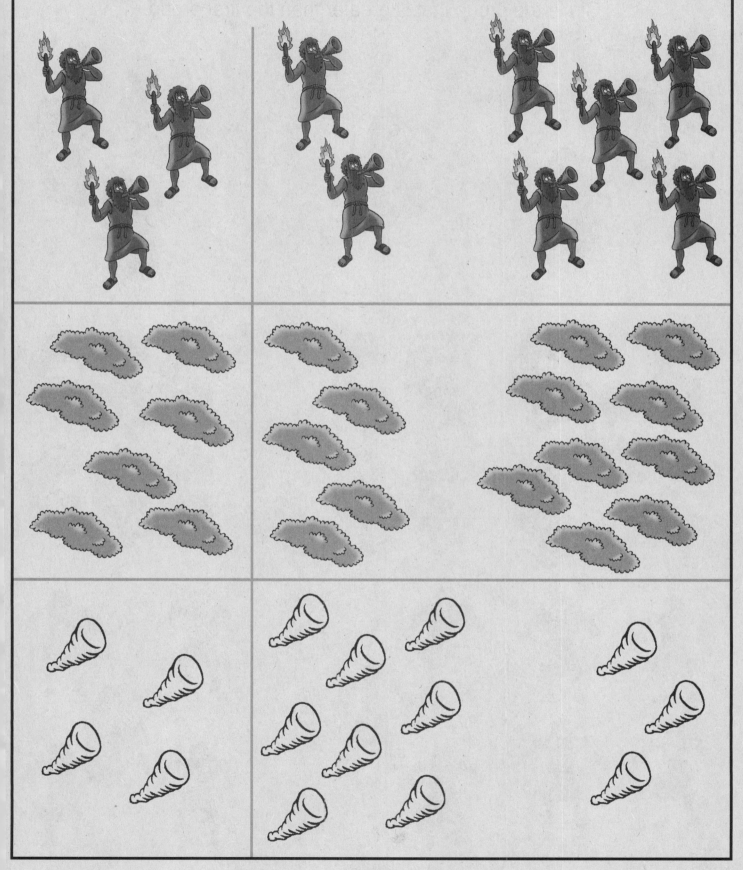

Super Samson

Samson's strength was greater than the Philistines.
Circle the group that is greater than the first group.

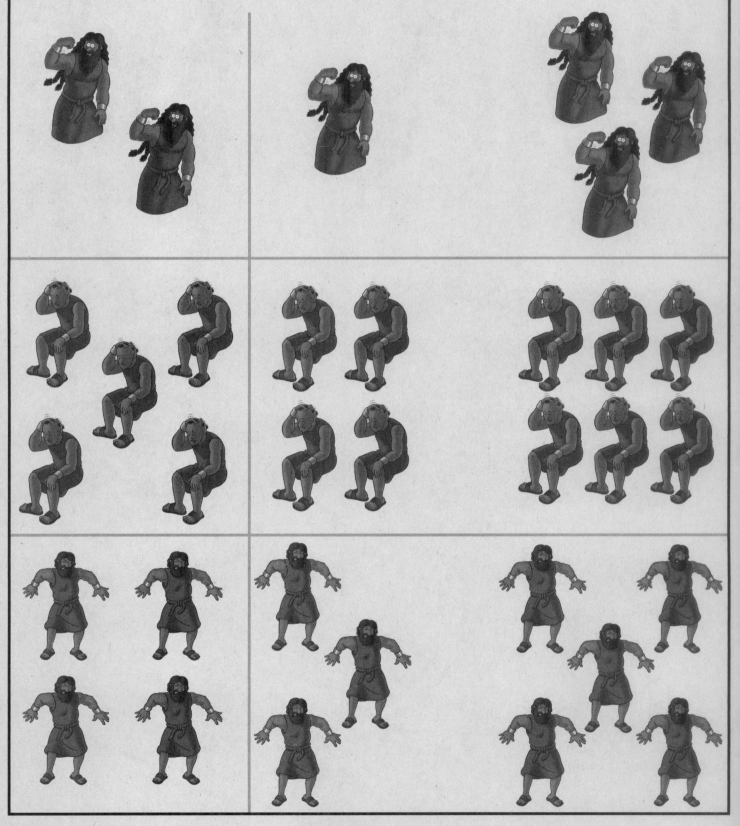

Same or Different

"I will go wherever you go," Ruth said.
Make an X on the pictures that are the same.

God's True Love

God loved the brand-new family. God loves you!
Connect the dots and color the picture.

Hannah's Prayer

Hannah prayed to God for a baby.
Draw a line to the picture that shows what happened.

Where To, Samuel?

Hannah brought Samuel to live at the tabernacle.
Lead Samuel to his bed in the tabernacle.

I Am Listening

Samuel heard God call. Samuel said, "I am listening."
Circle what you can hear.

Where Is Saul?

Saul tried to hide. Where is Saul? Draw Saul hiding.

Long Live Saul

The people found Saul. Draw Saul found by the people.

Saul Gets a Crown

God chose Saul to be the king.
Trace the shapes. Design and color a crown for Saul.

Next?

God said, "I look at the inside of a person. I look at the heart."
Color the hearts and the one that comes next in the pattern.
Use the code to color the hearts: 1= pink 2 = red 3 = purple

1 2 1 2 1 ♡

2 1 1 2 1 ♡

1 2 3 1 2 ♡

The Smallest

David was the smallest brother.
Circle the picture that is smaller than the first one.

Full of Love

David was filled with God's power.
Circle what is full. Make an X on what is empty.

Big, Bigger, Biggest

Goliath was much bigger than David!
Circle the picture that is bigger than the first one.

Too Heavy!

The armor was too heavy for David.
Draw a line to give the heavy things to Samson.

Which One?

David said, "God will be with me."
Find and circle the stone that hit the giant's forehead.

Friends

Jonathan and David were best friends.
Read the clues. Draw a line from the names to the correct person.
Clues: Michal is Jonathan's sister.
Jonathan is wearing a cape.

Michal   Jonathan   David

D-D David

David became king. Trace D. Circle the pictures whose names begin with the D sound like David.

D

Donkey

Balcony

King David

Feather

Desk

Sing Praise

David wrote songs about God called psalms. He wrote,
"The Lord is my shepherd." Look at the picture. Put an X on the
shepherd. Circle some things people need to live. Color the grass green.
Color the water blue.

Yay, David!

The Lord is my shepherd, I will not be afraid.
Draw David's face to show that he is not afraid.

God Is Good

The Lord is my shepherd. God's goodness and love will
follow me all the days of my life.
Trace the path from the lamb to David.

Being Different Is OK

King Solomon wants to know the difference.
Circle the picture that is different.

Count on God

King Solomon spoke 3,000 proverbs and wrote 1,000 songs.
Trace 3. Trace 1. Trace 0. Write the numbers.

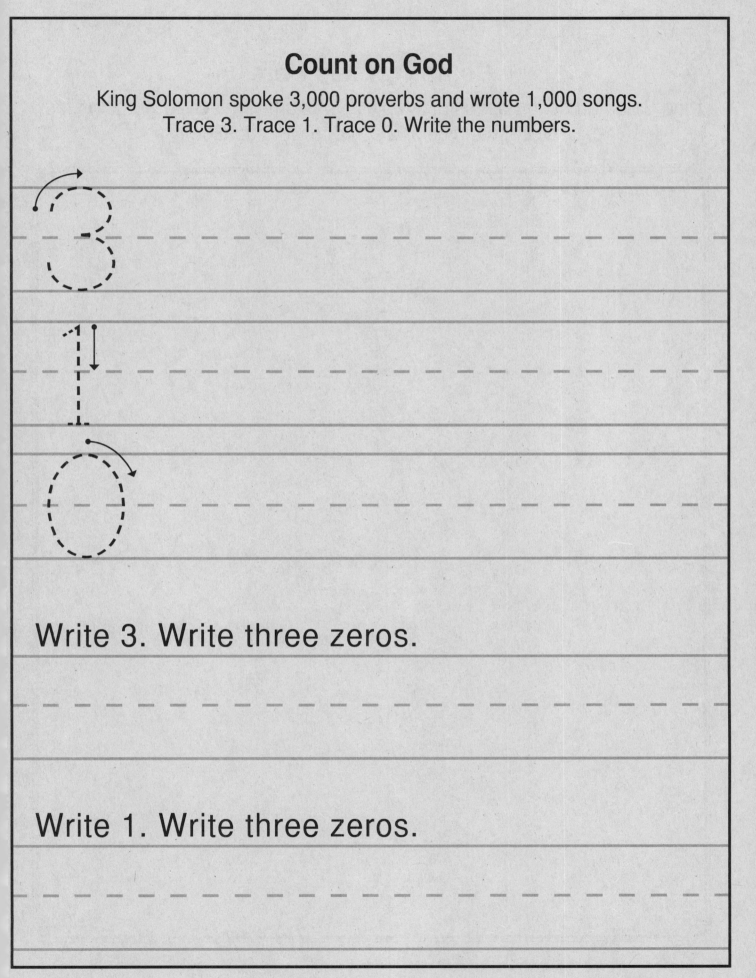

Write 3. Write three zeros.

Write 1. Write three zeros.

Come Worship Here

King Solomon built a beautiful temple. It was a new place to worship God.
Design and color a place to worship God.

God Is Good to Elijah

God took care of Elijah in the desert.
Circle all the things God added to the desert for Elijah.

Thanks, God!

Because the woman took care of Elijah,
she could make more and more bread.
Circle the picture that is more than the first one.

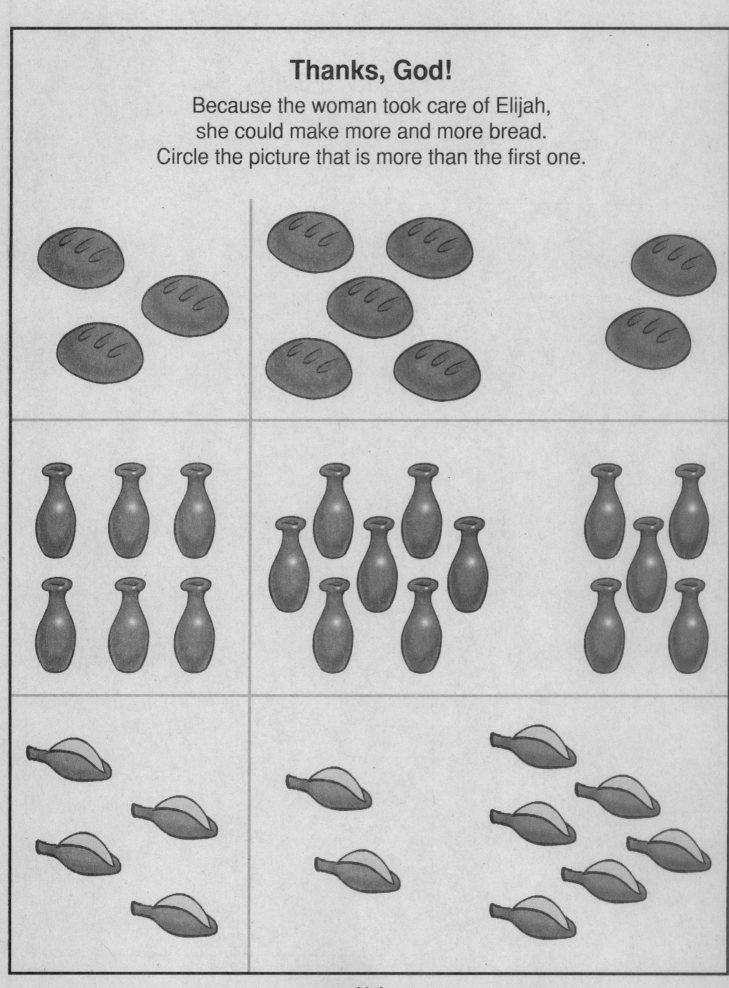

Counting on God

Baal is not God. Baal could not help the people.
Count the blocks. Trace the numbers. Write the number of blocks.

Build It Up

Elijah built an altar to God.
Draw a line to show which block goes next.

Prophets Are Helpers

Elijah and Elisha told people about God's love.
Color the prophet on the left. (←)

All from God

God gave the widow many pots of oil.
Put a check on the pots of oil that are between other pots.

Thanks, Says Elisha

Elisha's friends gave him food.
Circle what is on the table. Put an X on the food not on the table.

Trace Around

Elisha's friends gave him a room.
Trace the rectangles. Color the picture.

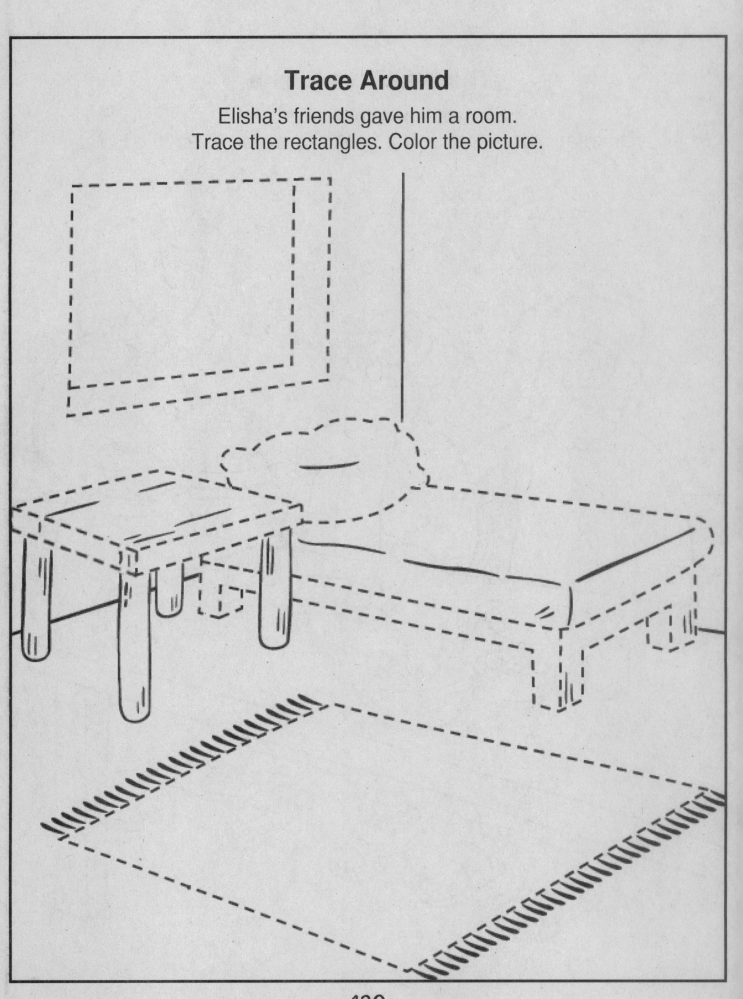

Connect With God

God loved Elisha's friends. God loves you. Connect the dots.

Naaman Needs God

Naaman went in the water. God made Naaman well.
Circle what is in the water.

The Book of Law

The priest found the Book of Law.
Draw a line from the scroll to where it was found.

Yes, God!

The people made a promise to obey God's laws.
Circle the picture that shows why this happened.

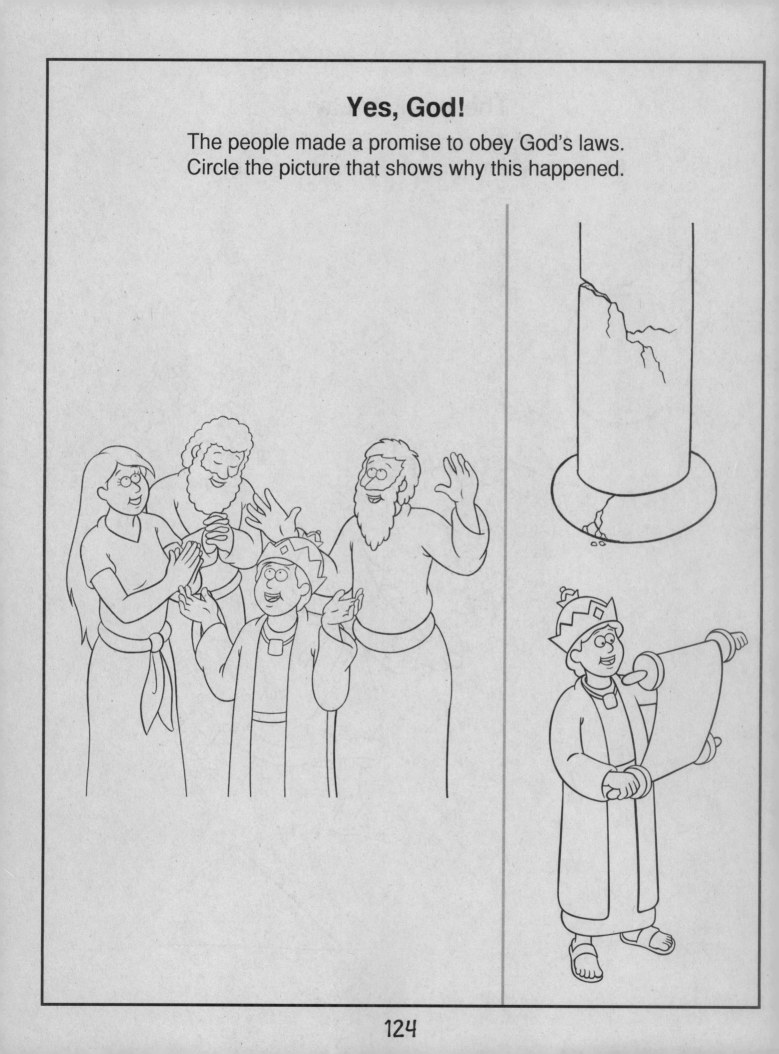

Good Plans

Esther had a plan. Draw a line to match each person with their plan.

Just Say NO

The king said, "Everyone must bow down to the golden statue."
Put an X on the men who bowed down. Circle the men who are standing up.

Love Only God

The king put the men who would not bow down in the furnace.
The furnace was extra hot, but God did not let the men get hurt.
Color the thermometer to show how hot. Color the flames.

10	20	30	40	50	60	70	80	90	100	110	120

Obey and Pray

Daniel prayed to God, not to the king. Draw a picture of your prayer to God.

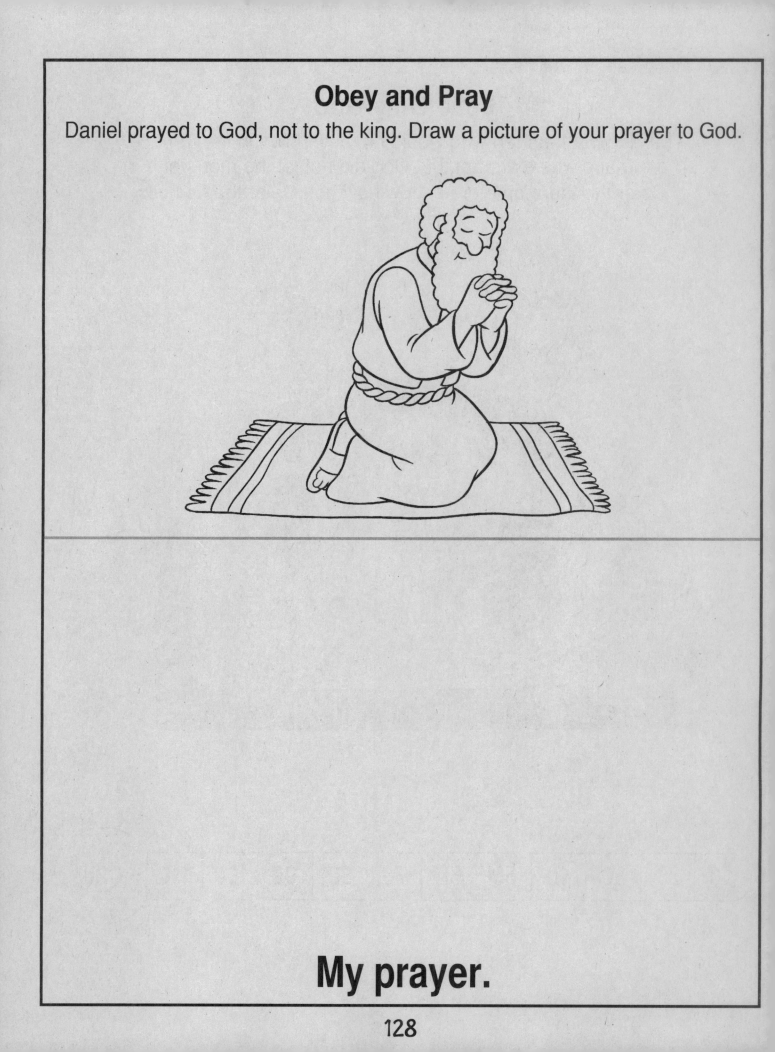

My prayer.

Trace the Ls

The king threw Daniel in the lions' den. God sent an angel to protect Daniel. Trace and write L. Circle the pictures whose names begin with the L sound like lion.

Lamp

Moon

Rug

Lion

Legs

Logs

Jonah's Search

Jonah tried to run away from God. He got on a boat.
Find and circle the words in the puzzle below.

SINK   STORM   STOP

SAIL   SEA   SAILOR

M J N X V V V K N

X R H N T N N P

S T O P E A I G

W B P T F L S L

J Z M N S T I E

S R O L I A S A

V E J W S P P Y

Z C A R B Q B C

Inside and Out

The sailors threw Jonah into the sea. A big fish swallowed Jonah.
Circle who is inside. Put an X on who is outside.

First, Next, Last

Jonah obeyed God. He told the people to stop doing bad things. God forgave the people. Write 1 under what happened first. Write 2 under what happened next. Write 3 under what happened last.

An Angel's Job

The angel said to Mary, "You will have a son. Name him Jesus."
Draw a line from the angel to its shadow.

Yes!

Mary said, "Yes." Trace and write Y, E, and S. Trace YES.

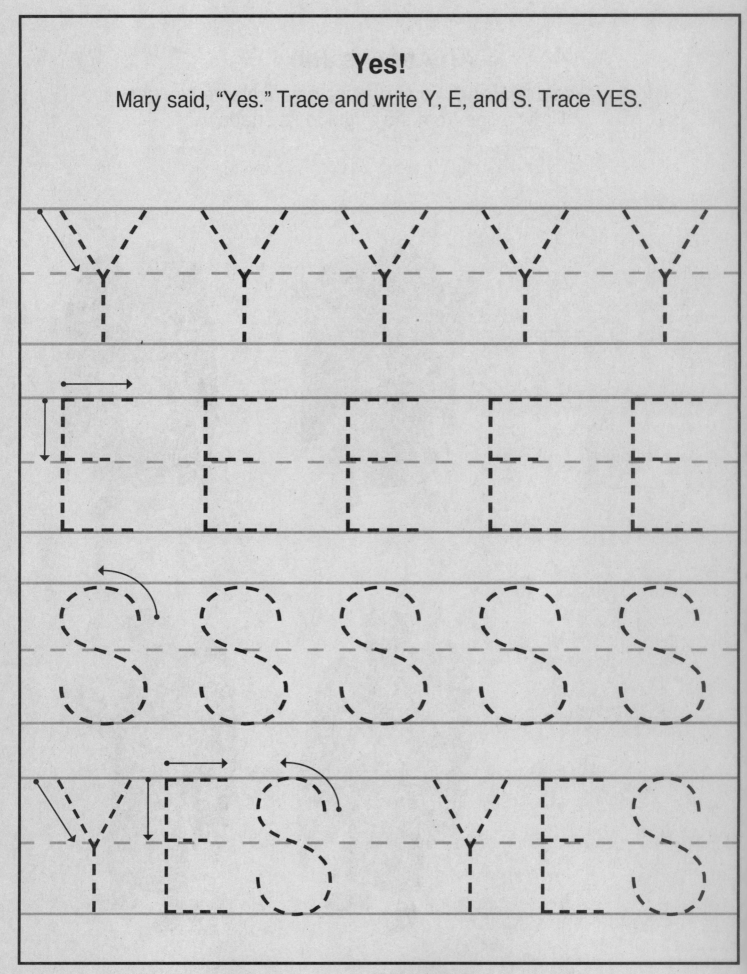

God Is Good

God loved Mary and Joseph. God loves you. Connect the dots.

Let's Go To Bethlehem

Mary and Joseph went to Bethlehem. Trace their path.

Jesus Is Here

Jesus is born! Trace and write J. Trace Jesus. Color the picture.

The C Sound

The animals gathered near the new baby.
Trace C. Circle the pictures whose names begin with the
same beginning sound as Cow.

Sheep

Crab

Cat

Jellyfish

Cow

Far, Far Away

The shepherds were watching the sheep. Far above, the sky filled with God's light. Circle what is far from the shepherds.

Number 6

Angels sang the joyful news of Jesus. Trace 6. Write 6.
Circle the groups of six.

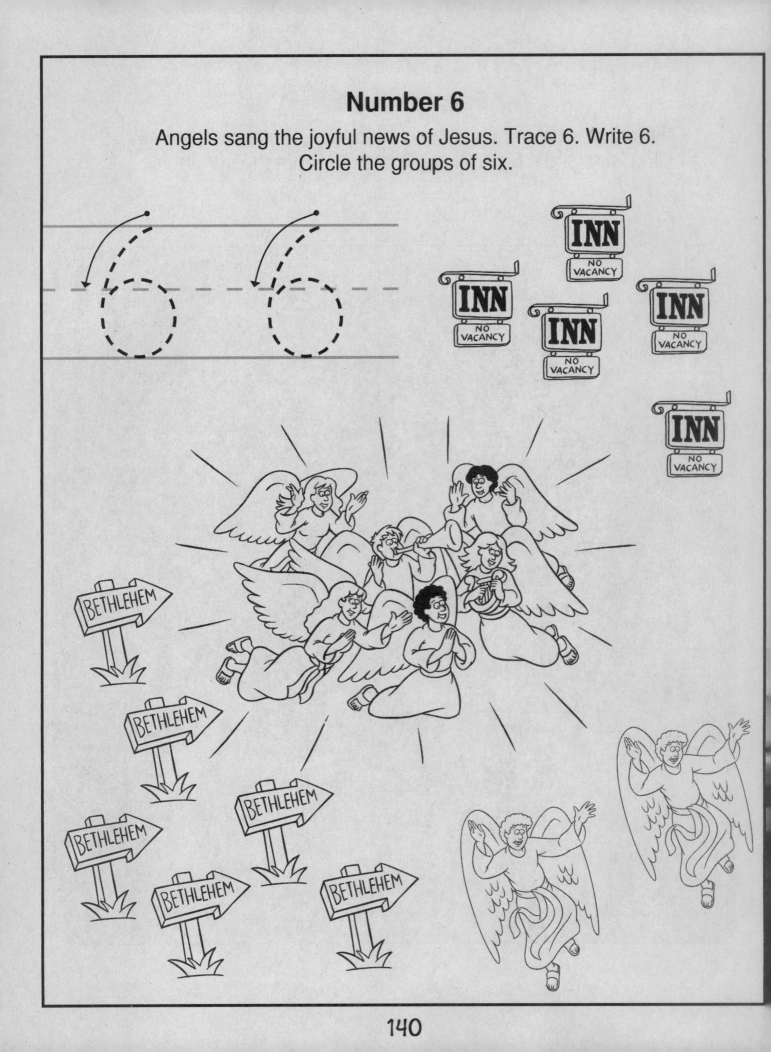

Makes a Difference

Anna and Simeon knew Jesus was the Savior. They could tell
Jesus was different. Circle the pictures that are different from the first one.

Stars

The special star in the sky was a sign from God.
Trace and color the stars. Circle the number of stars.

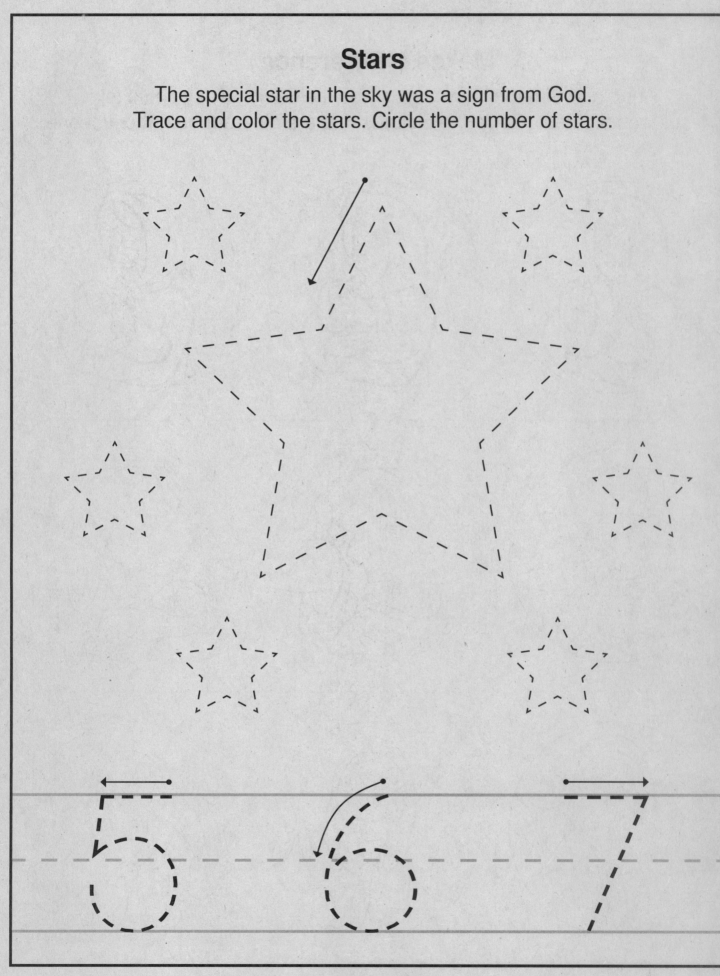

Follow Him

The wise men followed the star.
Put an X on the ones who are following in the picture.

A Good Gift

The wise men brought gifts for Jesus.
What can you give to Jesus? Draw your gift in the box.

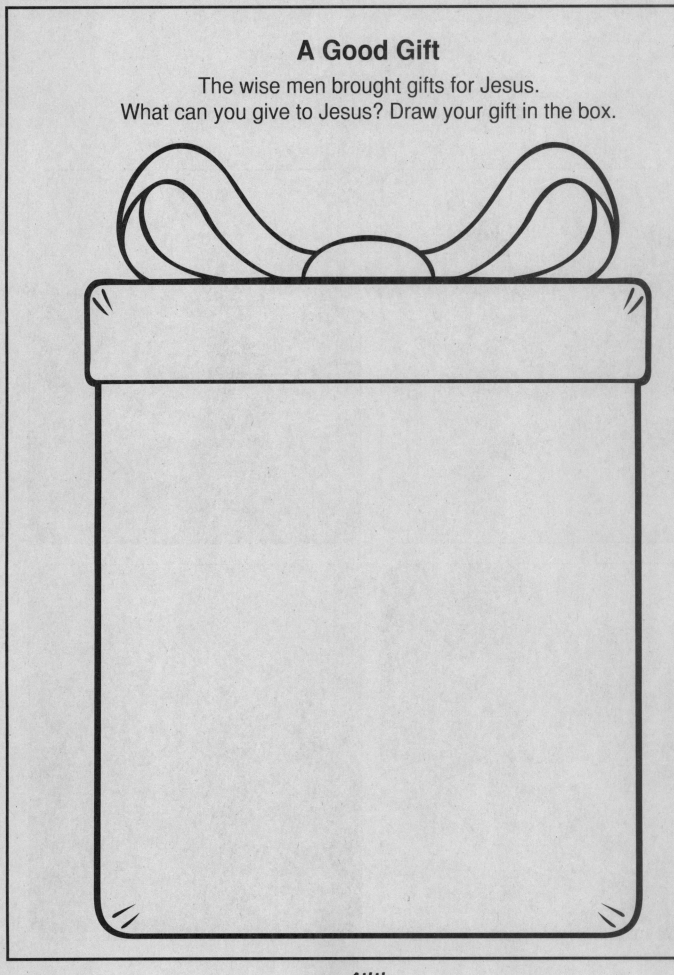

Opposites

An angel told the wise men to go home the opposite way.
Draw a line to connect two opposites.

Angry King Herod

King Herod was angry. "I am the only king!" he yelled.
Circle the angry faces.

Finish It

God's angel said for Joseph, Mary, and Jesus to go to Egypt. They would be safe in Egypt. Draw a line to show which piece completes each pyramid.

Bigger!

Jesus grew up in the small village of Nazareth. Every year, his family went to Jerusalem. Jerusalem was much bigger than Nazareth.
Circle the group that is bigger.

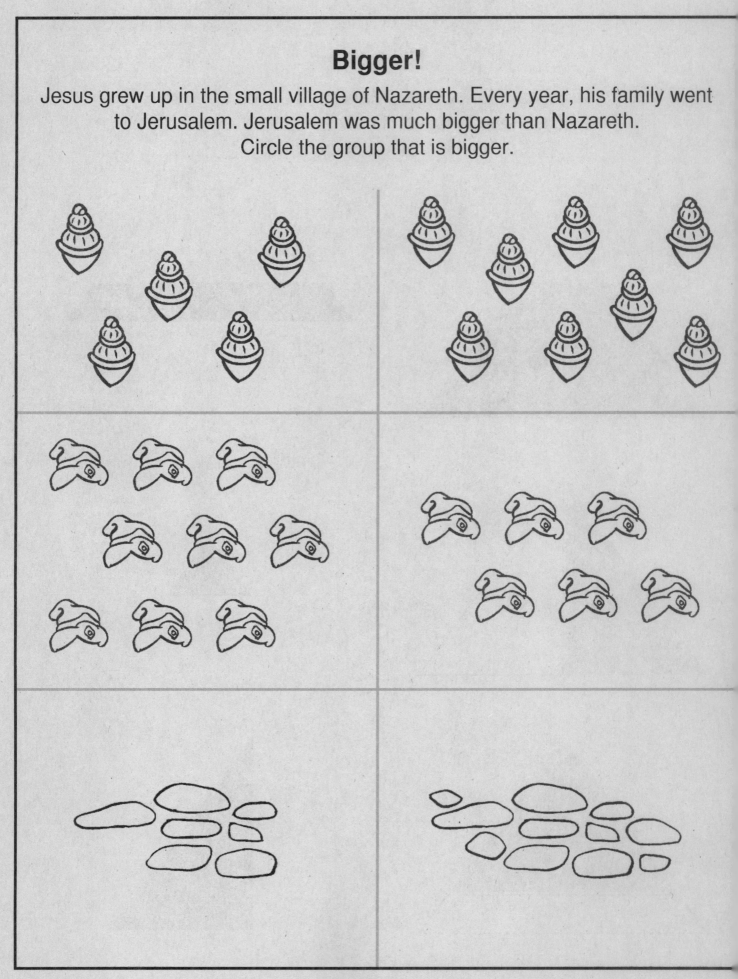

Twelve ... 12

When Jesus was twelve, they went to Jerusalem.
Trace and write 12. Count twelve. Circle twelve.

Front and Back

It was time to go home. Jesus was not in front of the crowd or in back of the crowd. Circle the one who is in the front of the crowd. Put an X on someone in the back of the crowd.

My Father's House

Mary and Joseph found Jesus in the temple.
"I am in my Father's house," Jesus said. Which is the temple?
Read the clues. Circle the correct picture.

Clues: It cannot float.
It has a look-out on the roof.
It can not be folded up and carried.

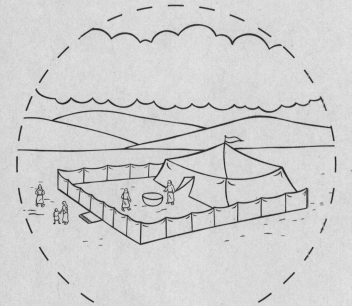

Nice Nine

John and Jesus were cousins. John ate bugs and honey.
Trace 9. Circle the groups of nine bugs.

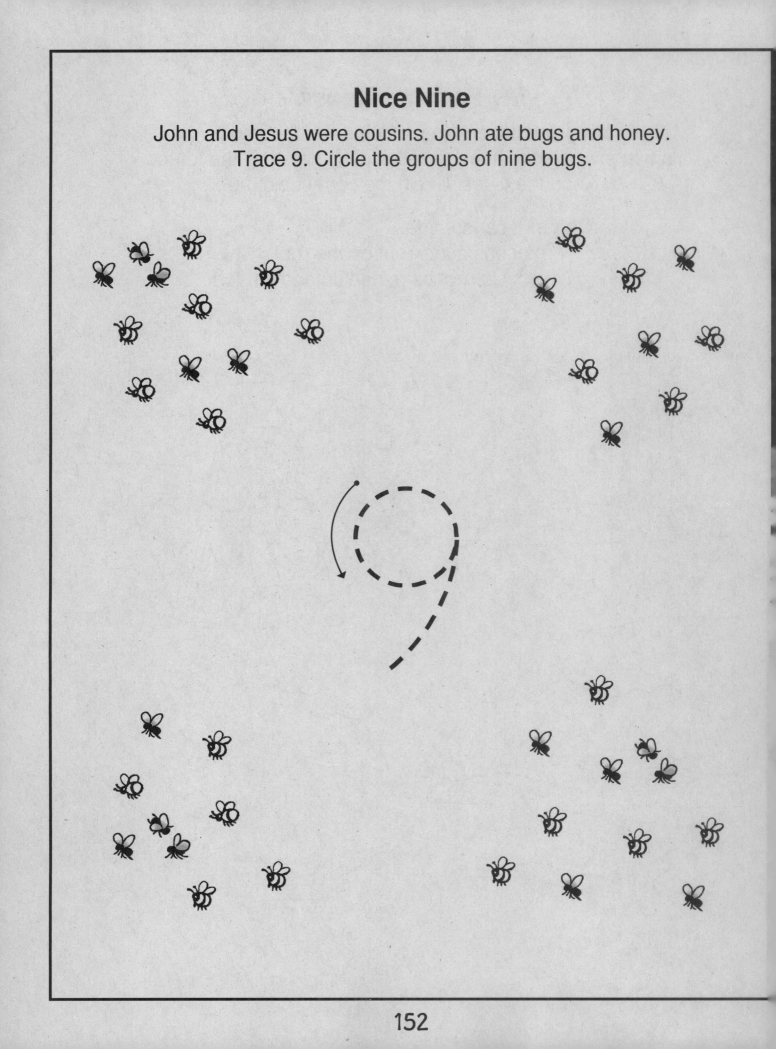

Search Out John

John told people about God.
Find the words and circle them in the puzzle below.

JOHN	TOLD	GOD
GOOD	KIND	HONEST

K I N D Y V V D

J Z D U Q Z O K

B T L I M O O Y

S Q O L G W U G

G H T N I Q J G

U O I C H X H N

R U D E P O M S

T S E N O H J Q

Blue Waters

John baptized the people in the blue water of the river.
Color the water blue.

Beside Him

Jesus stood beside the river. He asked John to baptize him.
Follow the directions below to show **beside**. Use a check (✔).

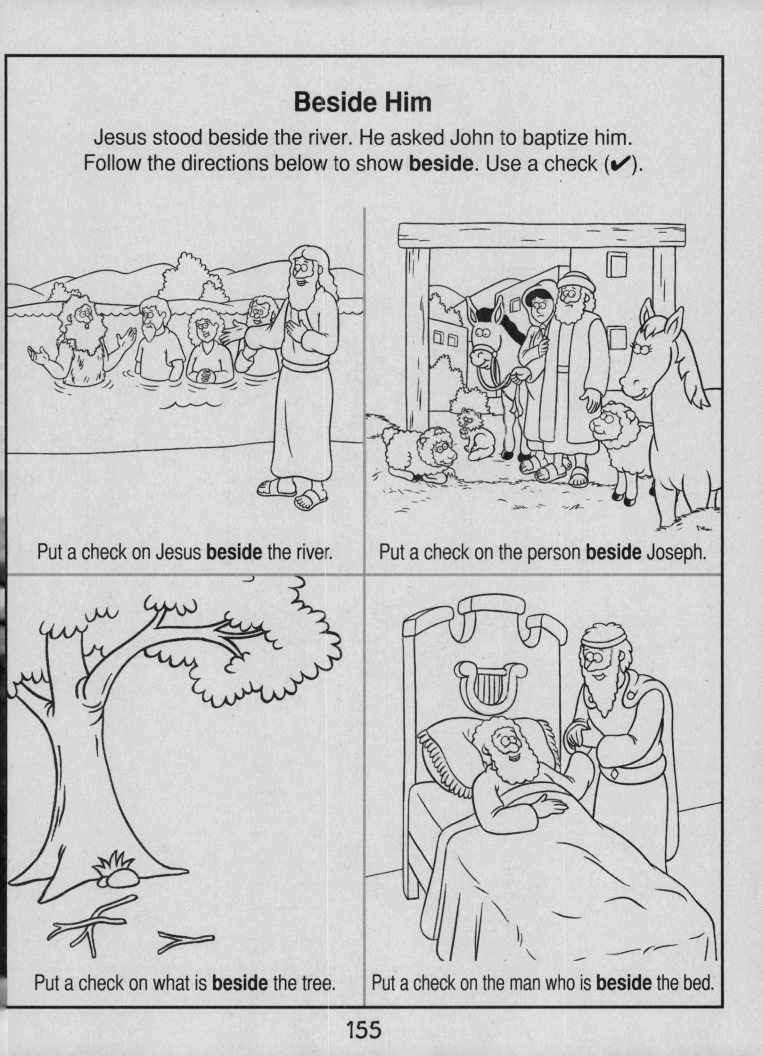

Put a check on Jesus **beside** the river.

Put a check on the person **beside** Joseph.

Put a check on what is **beside** the tree.

Put a check on the man who is **beside** the bed.

6 + 6 = 12

Jesus chose 12 disciples.
Count the disciples. Circle groups of 6. Trace the numbers.

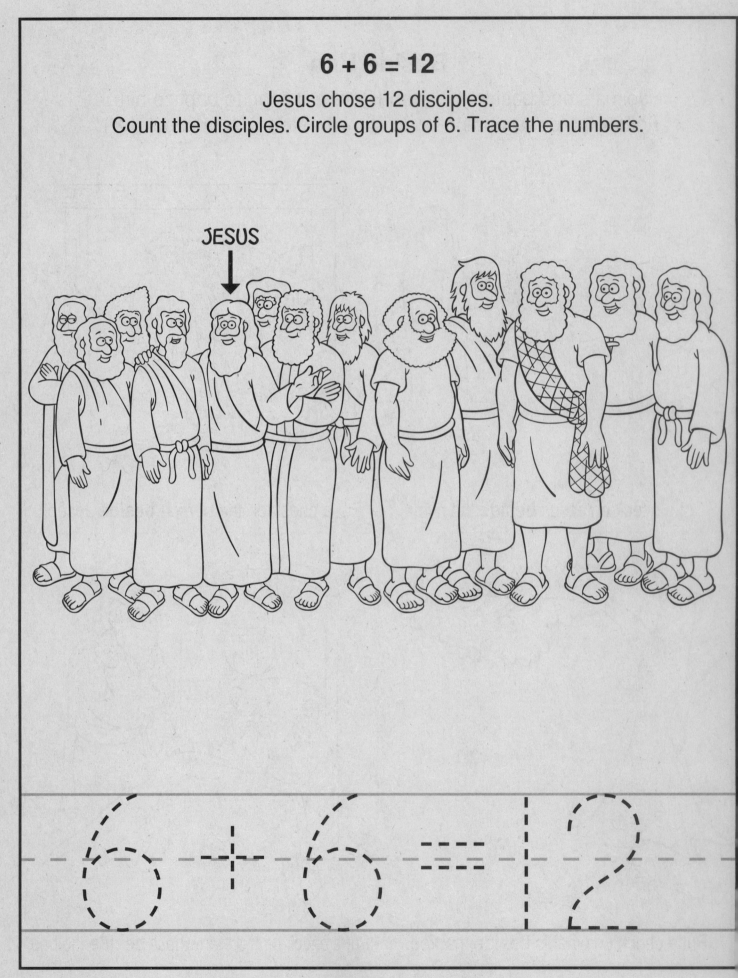

JESUS

Less

Jesus went to a wedding. There was not enough wine.
Circle the picture that has less.

Fill Them Up

Jesus said, "Fill up six jars of water."
Trace the shapes. Color them blue to fill them up.

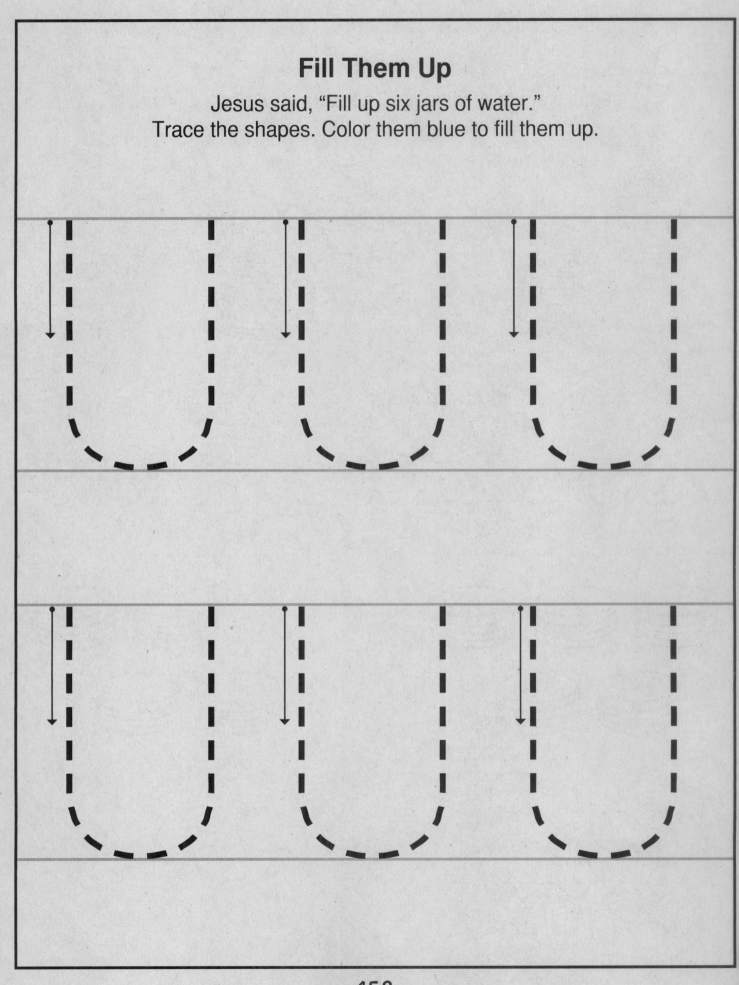

Which Is Last

The water became wine! The master said, "You have saved the best wine for last." Make an X on the last person.

Only God

This was Jesus' first miracle. Only God can do miracles.
Draw a picture of something only God can do.

Jesus Teaches

Jesus taught many people. Color the page.

Food from God

Jesus said, "God feeds the birds." God feeds people too.
Put an X on the food for people.

All from God

God dresses the flowers. God cares for people too.
Color the clothes for people.

Thank You, God

Jesus said, "Don't worry. God will take care of you."
Complete the prayer with your drawings.

Thank you, God, for food to eat.

My favorite food.

Thank you, God, for clothes to wear.

My favorite shirt.

Pray

Jesus taught the people how to pray. Trace and color
the frame for Jesus' prayer.

Our Father in heaven,

hallowed be your name,

your kingdom come,

your will be done

on earth as it is in heaven.

Give us today our daily bread.

Forgive us our debts,

as we also forgive our debtors.

And lead us not into temptation,

but deliver us from the evil one.

Amen

Bigger Than That

Jesus had not seen faith as big as the army captain's faith.
Circle the picture that is bigger than the first one.

You Can Do It!

The army captain was sure about Jesus.
Color by number. 1= yellow, 2 = gray, 3 = red, 4 = orange, 5 = brown, 6 = blue

In and Out

Many people wanted to see Jesus. They were inside and outside.
Circle who is **inside**. Put on X on who is **outside**.

Help and Heal

A man couldn't walk. His friends believed Jesus could heal him.
Trace H and write H. Find and circle the H words in the puzzle below.

HOUSE   HIM   HOLE
HEAL   HELP   HEAVEN

```
L  M  R  P  H  E  I  M
H  L  C  H  O  O  X  A
P  E  O  W  U  Q  Q  C
C  L  A  D  S  C  H  F
E  W  E  V  E  V  P  M
X  G  O  H  E  V  H  I
L  A  E  H  C  N  C  H
I  X  I  R  A  J  D  S
```

Down By Jesus

A man couldn't walk. His friends lowered him down to Jesus.
Draw an arrow (↓) on what is **down**.

All Well

Jesus forgave the man, and the man was made well!
Color the picture that shows *Jesus made the man well*.

A Strong Bridge

Jesus and his disciples wanted to cross the sea. Will a bridge help? Trace the rectangles. Use the rectangles to draw a bridge across the water.

Jesus Naps Too

The disciples and Jesus got into a boat. Jesus took a nap.
Trace the figure to complete the picture. Color the picture.

Wwwwwww

Waves splashed! Wind whipped! Trace and write W.

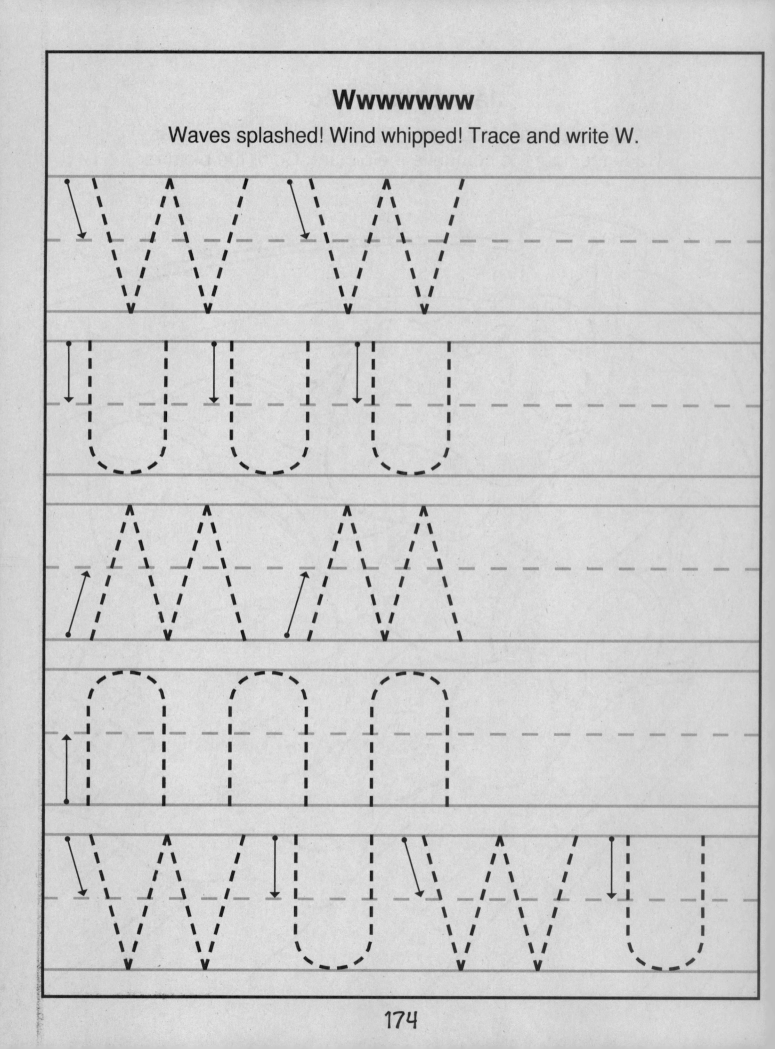

Stop!

Jesus told the storm to stop. The storm stopped.
Storm and calm are opposites. Draw a line to match the opposites.

Touching

When the woman touched Jesus, she was well. When Jesus touched the little girl, she was well. Circle the things you can touch.

For Real

Jesus said, "Your faith has made you well." Faith is knowing God is real.
Trace and write F. In the diamond, draw something you know is real.

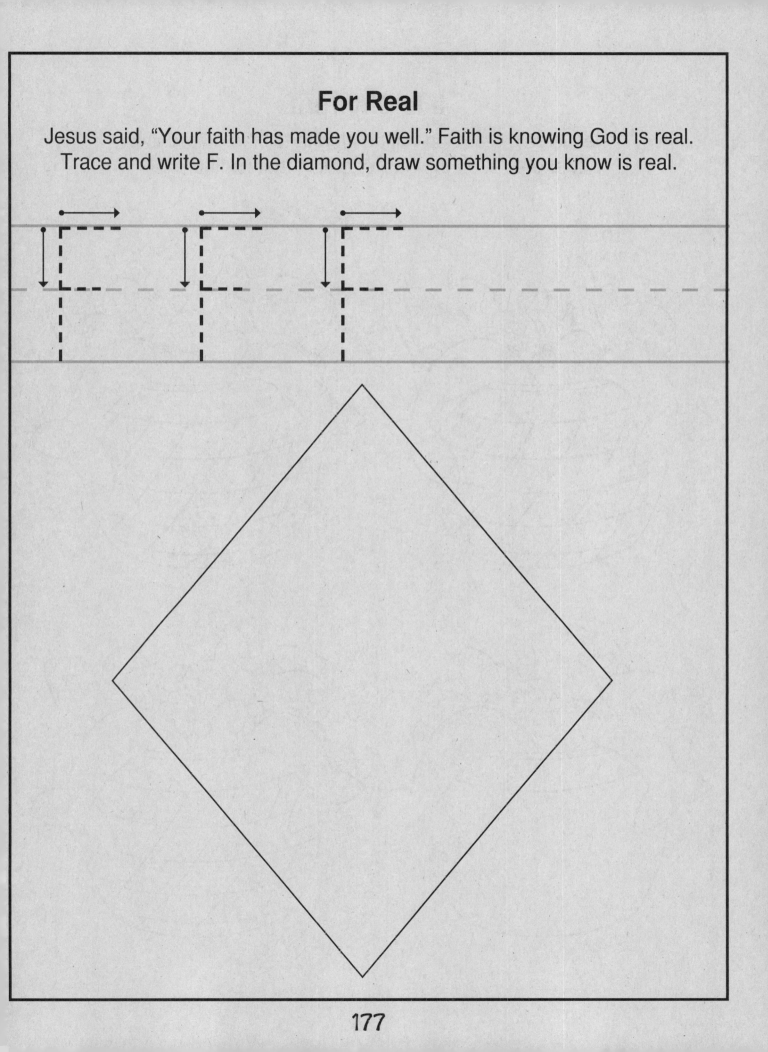

It Is Different

Jesus said that God will be able to tell the difference.
Make an X on the basket of fish that is different.

Heaven

Heaven is where God lives. Color the picture.

Big Boats

Jesus and his disciples got into a boat.
Trace and write B. Trace triangles to complete the boat.

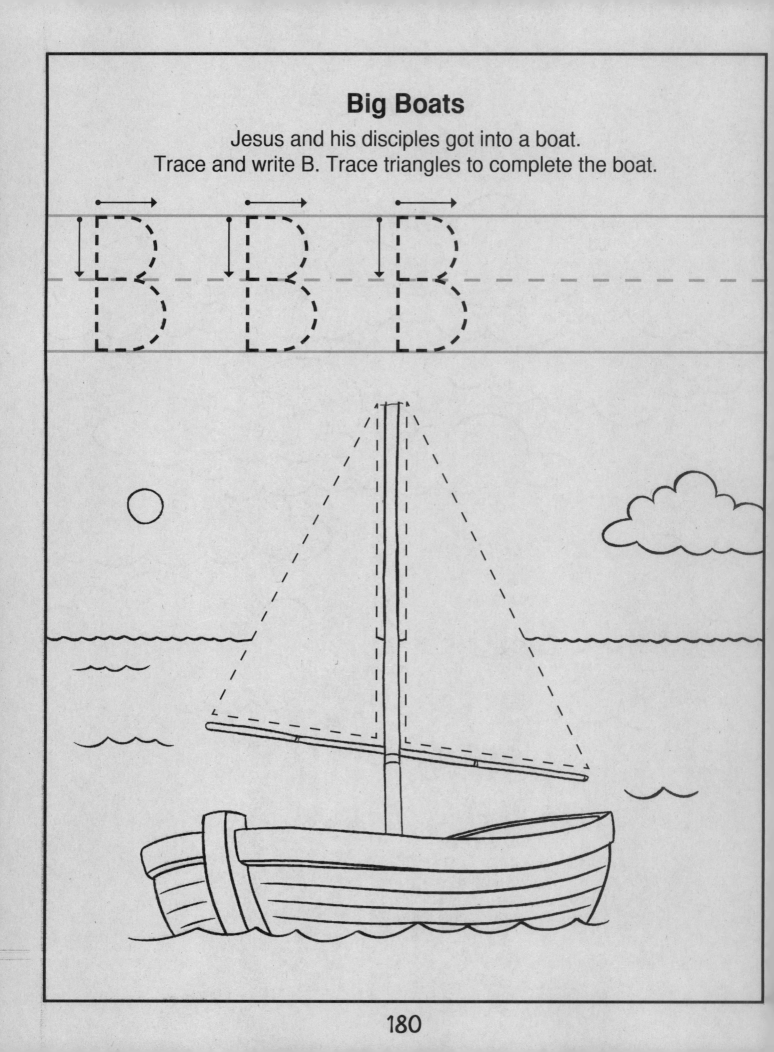

Lots of People

Five thousand people wanted to see Jesus.
Trace 5. Trace 0. Trace 5,000. Circle the groups of five.

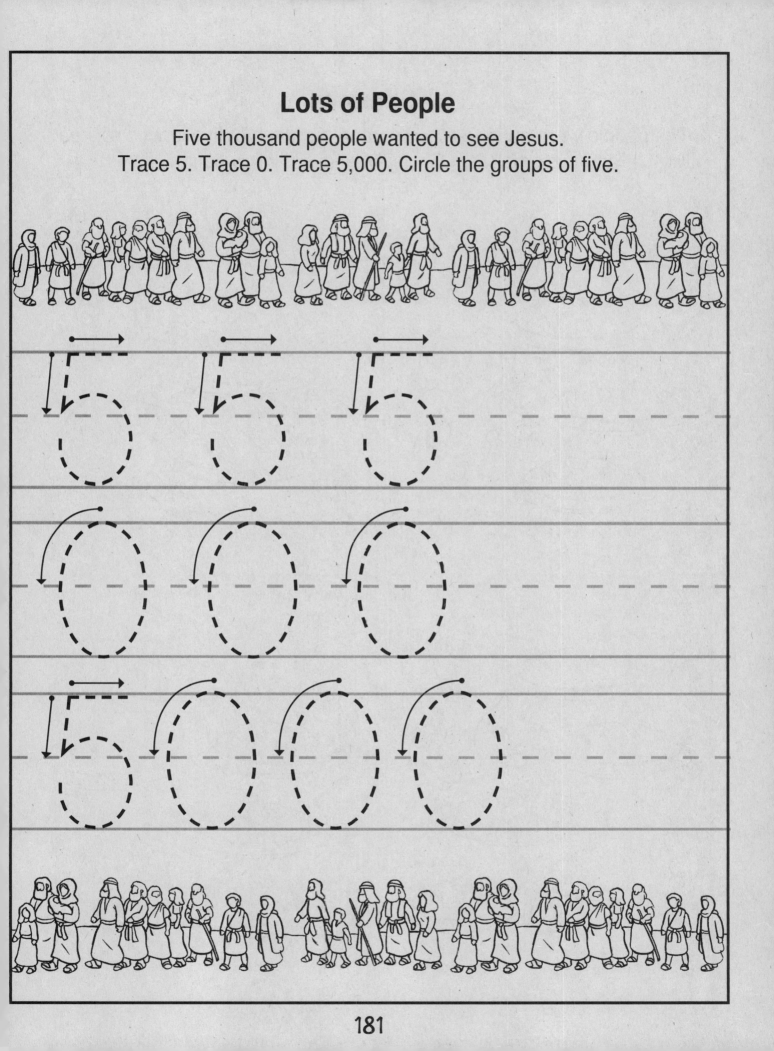

Sharing

The people were hungry. A boy shared his lunch of five loaves of bread and two small fish. Circle five loaves and two small fish.

Leftovers

Jesus blessed the loaves and fish. He gave thanks to God. Twelve baskets of food were left over! Circle twelve baskets.

Stay and Pray

Jesus wanted to stay and pray. The disciples went ahead.
Circle who is going ahead in each picture.

Far Away

Far away, Jesus saw a storm on the lake.
Make an X on what is far in each picture.

It Is Jesus

Jesus walked on the water. The disciples thought it was a ghost!
Connect the dots to show Jesus. Color Jesus.

Peter Tries Too

Peter said, "Let me walk out to you." When Peter became afraid, he started to sink. Trace and write P. Color the picture.

What Do You See?

The blind man cannot see. Circle what God gave us so that we can see.
Draw the eyes of someone in your family.

Jesus Helps

Jesus spit on the ground and made mud with it. Put an X on the place where mud would be found. Draw a drop of water on the dry ground.

Making Mud

Jesus put mud on the man's eyes. Circle the mud on the blind man's eyes.
Draw a face. Draw the mud on the eyes that Jesus put on the blind man.

On and Off

Jesus said, "Go and wash off the mud."
Draw a line to connect on and off pictures.

See!

The blind man could see!
Listen for words that rhyme with see and draw a line to them.

BEE

WE

CAT

KNEE

CAKE

TREE

What Is Next?

It was time to pay the temple tax. Jesus paid the tax.
Draw a line to connect the pictures to show what happened next.

It Is Enough

Jesus gave Peter enough. Circle the picture that is the same as the first picture.

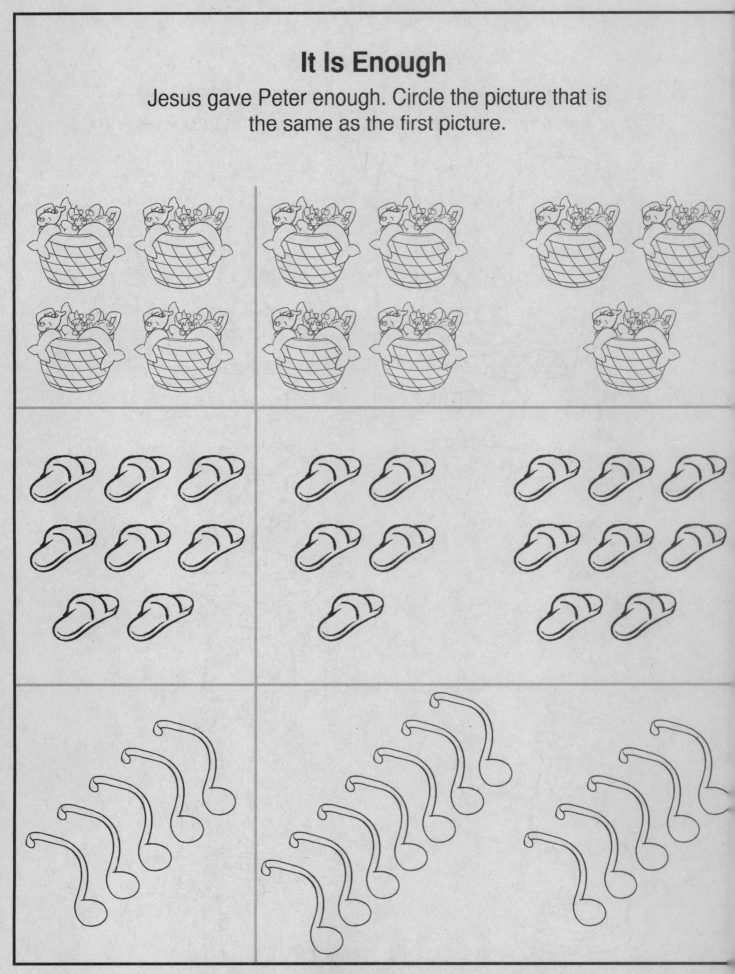

Where?

In whose mouth did Peter find the coin that was just enough?
Read the clues. Circle the right picture.

1. It is not furry.
2. It eats worms.
3. It likes to swim.

A Good Neighbor?

Who is my neighbor? Put the pictures in order to see a good neighbor.
Write 1 by what happened first. Write 2 by what happened next.
Write 3 by what happened last.

All Better

The good neighbor said, "Take good care of him until I return."
Draw a picture for the man who got hurt, to help him feel better.

Care for the Sick

God cares for people when they are sick. Trace the rectangles to make a bed and pillow. Draw someone in the bed. Draw and color a blanket.

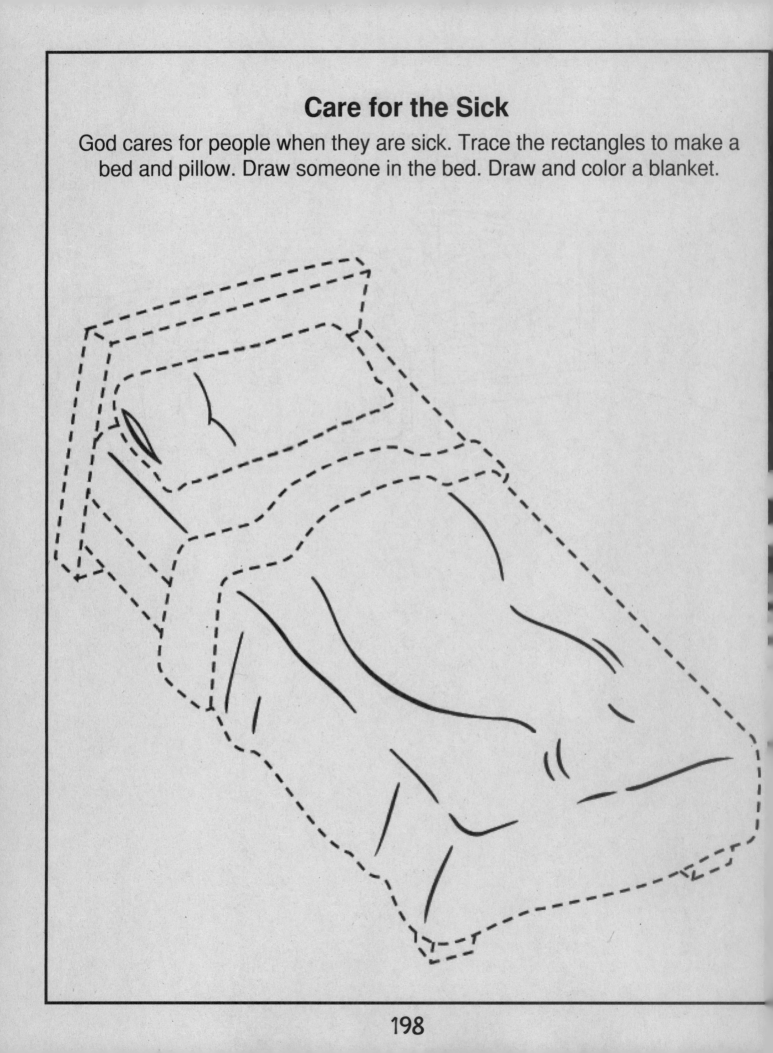

Jesus' Three Friends

Mary, Martha, and their brother Lazarus were friends with Jesus.
Trace 3. Write 3. Circle the groups of three.

Busy Day

Jesus came to visit. Martha was very busy.
Circle the tools Martha used for her work that day.

Sit and Listen

Mary sat and listened. Trace the squares and rectangles. Color the rug.

Near to Jesus

Jesus said, "Come near and listen to me. That is the best."
Put an X on what is near Jesus.

How Many?

Read the questions. Jesus told the people a story or parable.
Write the number of how many.

1. How many children?   1   2   3

2. How many women?   2   3   4

3. How many men?   7   8   9

4. How many pets?   1   2   3

Missing Number

A shepherd watches over his sheep. He counts them.
Look at each row. Which number is missing? Write the missing number.

1 2 ☐ 4 5

3 ☐ 5 6 7

4 5 6 ☐ 8

6 7 ☐ 9 10

More and More

Jesus said every sheep matters. One matters.
Circle the group that is one more than the first group.

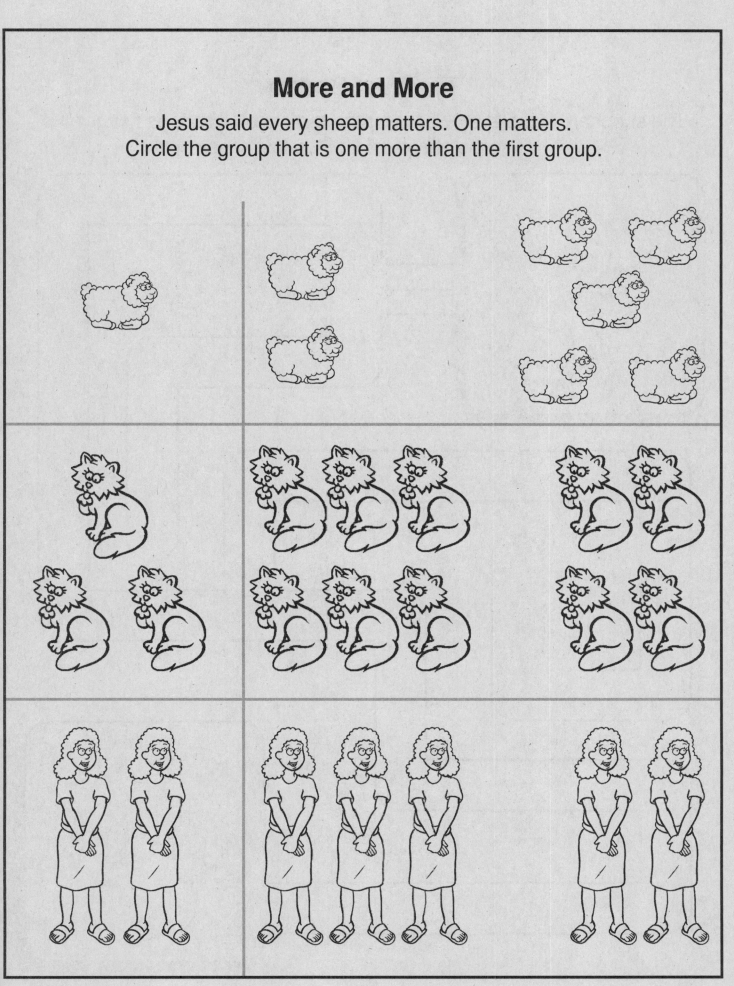

The Lost Sheep

The shepherd looks everywhere for the lost sheep. He does not give up.
Help the shepherd find the lost sheep.

We Belong

Jesus and his sheep belong together.
Draw a line to connect what belongs together.

Hooray!

Jesus said, "When a person comes back to God, God celebrates!"
Use many colors to fill the sky with fireworks!

Pick the Pairs

Jesus told a parable about two sons. A pair is two. Circle the pairs.

Match Them Up

The father and brothers worked hard on the farm.
Draw a line to connect the workers to their tools.

Going Far

One son didn't want to work. He wanted to go far away. Circle what is far.

His Money

The son asked his father for his share of the family money.
Look at the picture. Find and circle the money. Color the picture.

Less and Less

Soon the brother had no money.
Circle the group that has less than the other.

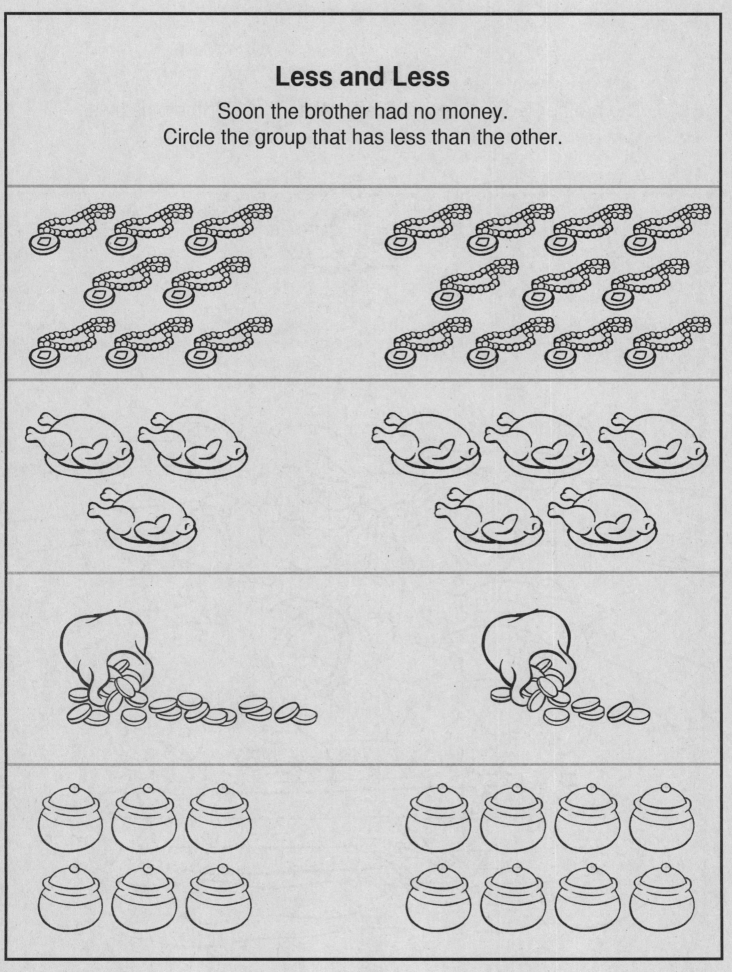

Pink Pigs

The brother fed the pigs. Trace P. Write P. Color the pigs pink.

G is for Good

The brother was hungry. The pig's food looked good! Good begins with G. Circle the pictures with the same beginning sound as *good*.

Rock

Goblet

Grain

Gecko

Girl

Stool

Mouse

Home, Sweet Home

The son wanted to go home. Help him find his way home.

Time to Celebrate

The father said, "My son was lost, but now he is found!"
They had a big party! Trace the triangles to make party hats.
Color them. Draw the faces of friends to wear the hats.

Finish This

God is full of love and joy when people who are lost come back to him. Part of the picture is missing. Draw a line to connect the piece that will make it whole again.

One to Ten

Jesus met ten sick men. Their bodies were covered in sores.
Count 1–10. Trace the numbers.

Heal Us, Lord

"Jesus, please heal us!" the sick men shouted.
Trace *heal*. Circle the words that rhyme with heal.

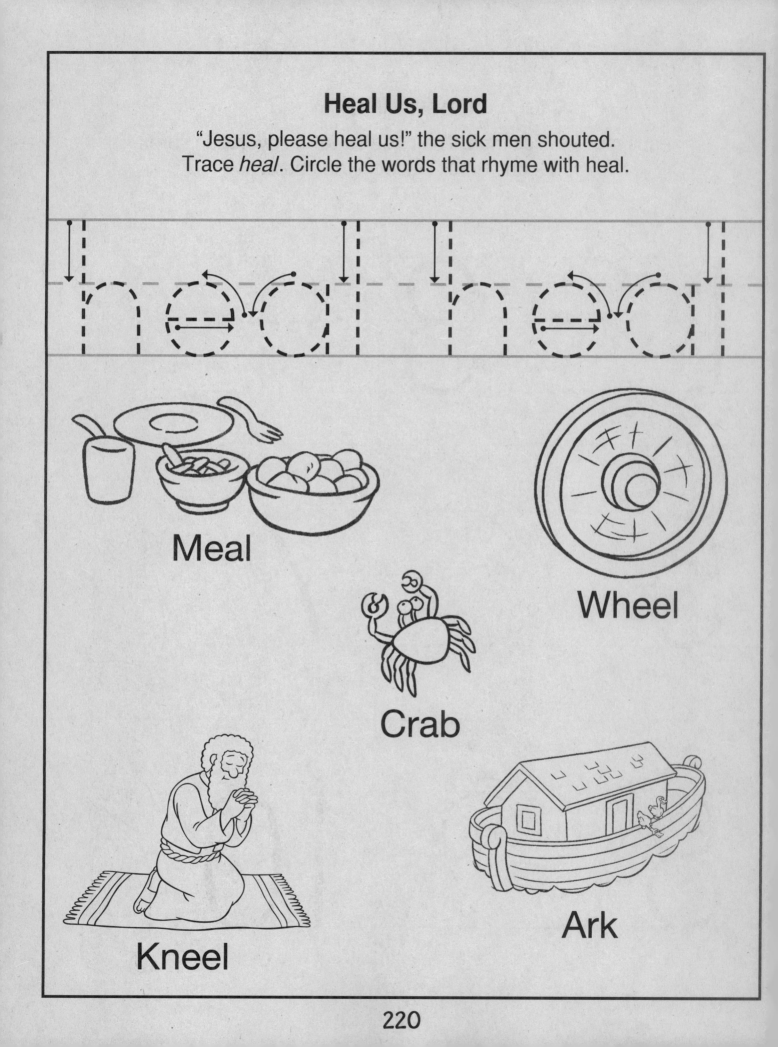

heal heal

Meal

Wheel

Crab

Kneel

Ark

X It Out

While the sick men were walking, Jesus healed them.
Put an X on what doesn't belong to the sick men anymore.

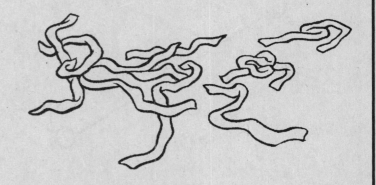

Thank You, Jesus

Only one man went back to thank Jesus.
Trace the path that goes from 1 to 8 to bring the man back to Jesus.

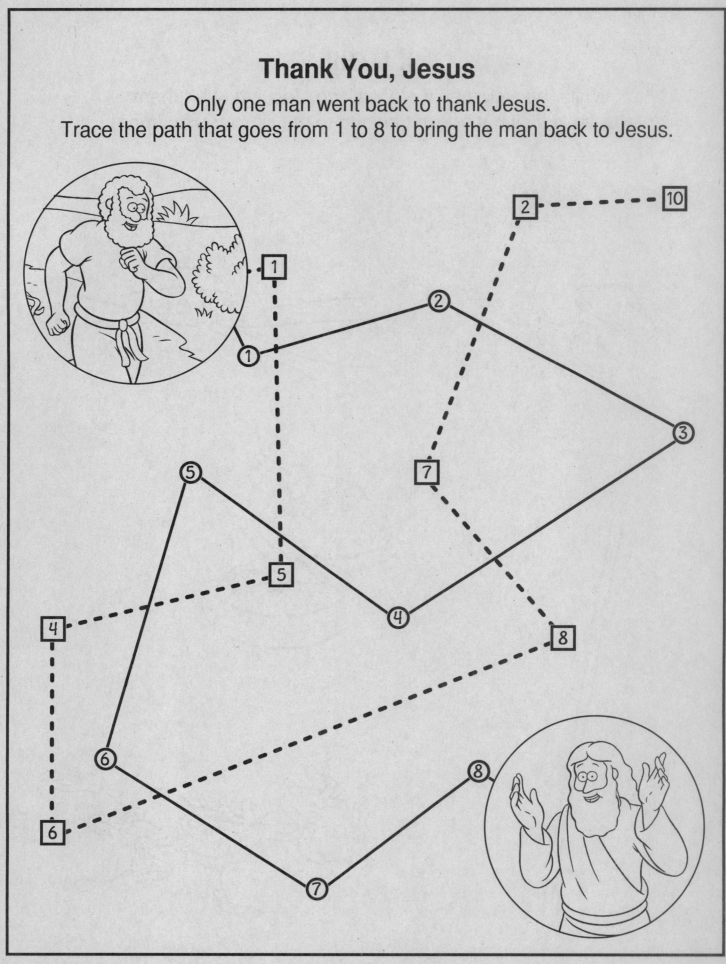

Remember to Say Thanks

"Thank you!" the man said to Jesus.
Thank Jesus for one of his gifts. Draw a picture of that gift.

Thank You, Jesus.

Children Love Jesus

The children loved to spend time with Jesus. Circle who belongs with Jesus.

Where Is Jesus?

The disciples said, "Jesus is too busy." The disciples stood between Jesus and the children. Trace a rectangle. Draw rectangles around who stood between Jesus and the children.

Like Children

Jesus said the disciples should be like whom?
Read the clues. Circle the correct pictures.

1. They like to play.
2. They are not grown up.
3. They love Jesus.

Blessings Left and Right

Jesus blessed the children on the left and on the right. Draw a left arrow (←) on the children to the left of Jesus. Draw a right arrow (→) on the children to the right of Jesus.

Short Stuff

Zacchaeus was short. He wanted to see Jesus.
Put an X on who is shorter.

Come Down

Zacchaeus climbed up a tree. Jesus said, "Come down."
Draw an up arrow (↑) on what is up.
Draw a down arrow (↓) on what is down.

Coins for the King

Zacchaeus collected the tax money to give to the king. Nobody liked Zacchaeus. Count the coins. Trace the number of coins the king wants.

Happy Faces

Zacchaeus was happy when Jesus came to his house.
Circle the happy faces.

More Money

Zacchaeus promised Jesus he would give back the extra money he had taken. He would give back even more!
Circle the coins that are more than the number.

Come, Jesus!

Mary and Martha sent Jesus a message. "Come quickly!"
Find and circle the words in the puzzle below.

```
M  H  G  E  I  R  S  T  Z  A
J  G  J  O  I  U  P  V  A  L
U  E  M  A  R  T  H  A  O  S
W  H  S  A  E  M  D  V  S  D
I  N  Z  U  V  A  E  O  E  N
U  A  W  G  S  R  C  L  X  E
L  N  E  O  P  Y  J  E  E  I
C  B  V  L  Z  S  F  J  F  R
E  N  S  Q  W  Z  D  J  D  F
```

Patterns

Jesus did not go for two days. Circle the pattern that shows two days.

Different

Martha said, "It would have been different if you had been here."
Look at the pictures. Make an X on the one that is different.

Just Pray

Jesus prayed for Lazarus who had died.
Think of someone special. Draw a picture of a prayer for that person.

New Life

Jesus gave Lazarus new life! Color by number the picture of new life.

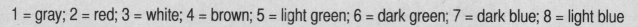

1 = gray; 2 = red; 3 = white; 4 = brown; 5 = light green; 6 = dark green; 7 = dark blue; 8 = light blue

A Visit

One evening, Jesus and his disciples went to visit Mary, Martha, and Lazarus. Circle the picture that shows evening.

Good Smells

Mary poured expensive perfume on Jesus' feet. It smelled sweet.
Circle what you can smell.

What Does It Cost?

Judas said Mary should not have wasted the perfume. He said it cost a lot.
What costs the most? Make an X on the answer.

Honor the Lord

Jesus said, "Mary did what was right. She honored me."
Use the code to color the page.

M = orange; J = purple; G = green; B = brown; S = blue; Y = yellow

241

Match Them

The disciples brought Jesus a donkey.
Match a person to what they brought.

A Big Welcome

Jesus rode to Jerusalem. A big crowd welcomed him!
Circle the picture that is bigger than the first one.

Hosanna

The crowd waved palm branches and shouted, "Hosanna!"
Color the palm branch green.

People Love Jesus

Many people were following Jesus. Some leaders did not like that.
Circle the picture that shows why this happened.

Count the Coins

In the temple, Jesus watched people drop money into the offering box. Count the coins. Circle the number that shows how many.

More Money Here

The rich people put a lot of money into the box.
Make an X on the picture that shows more.

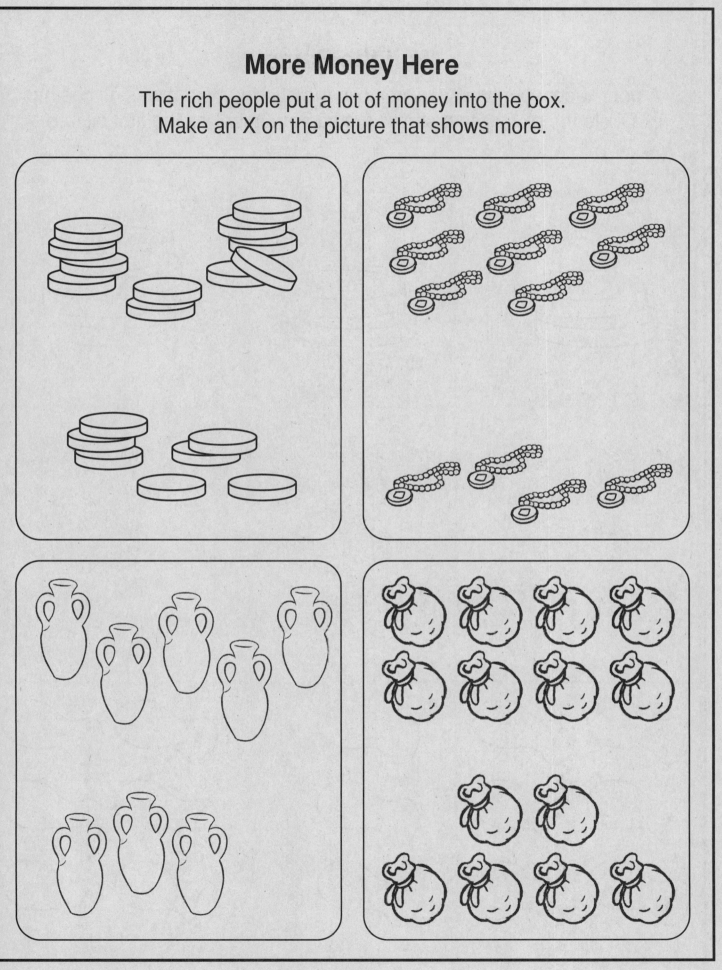

Is It the Same?

A poor widow put two small coins in the offering box. It was all she had. Circle the picture that shows the same number as the first picture.

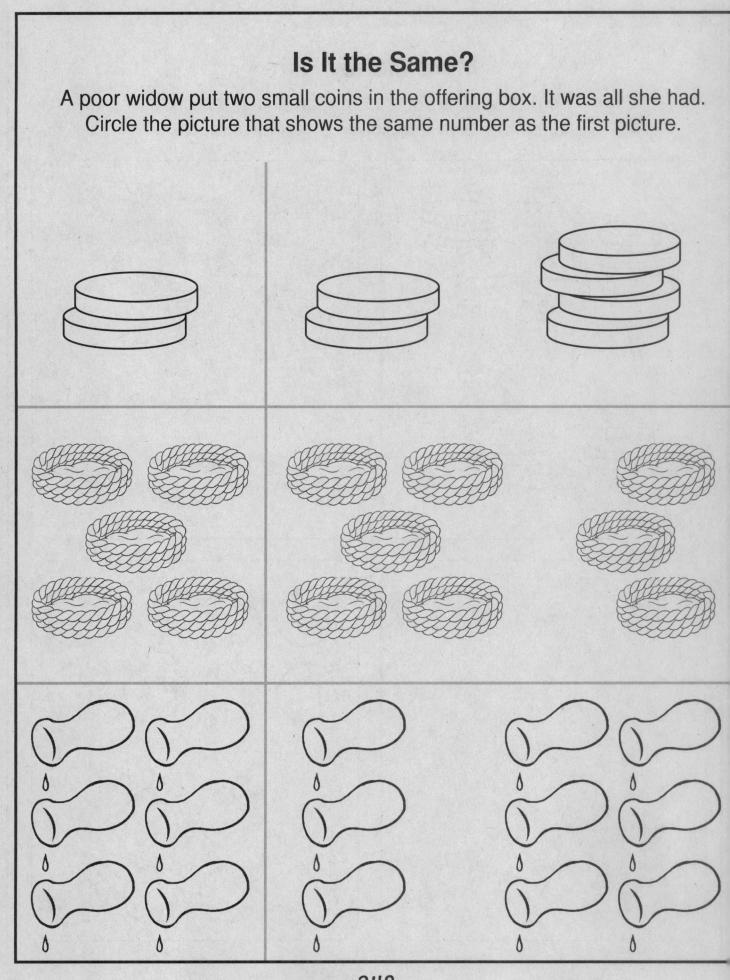

A Pattern of Giving

Jesus said the widow gave from her heart. Draw the shape that comes next.

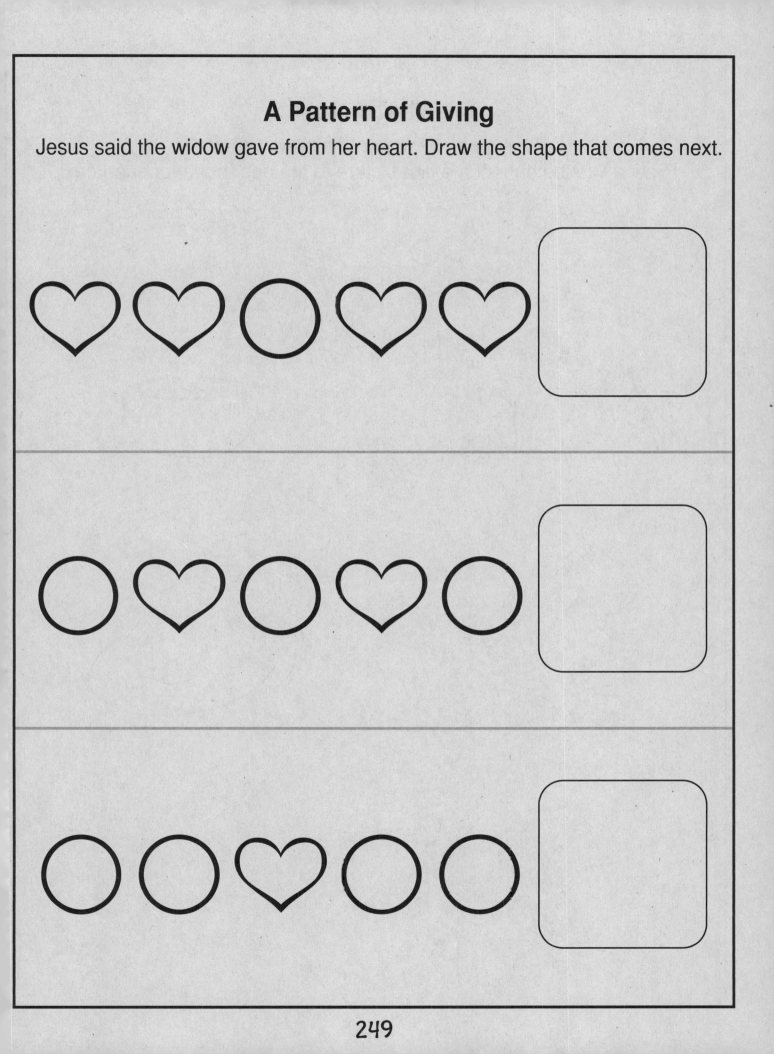

What's Next

After supper, Jesus filled a bowl with water.
Draw a line to connect the first picture to the one that happened next.

Pairs of Feet

Jesus washed and dried the disciples' feet, one by one.
Circle the pairs of feet Jesus washed.

What Belongs

Jesus said to Peter, "I must wash your feet for you to belong to my kingdom." Circle what belongs in the picture.

Love and Serve

"Wash each other's feet," Jesus said. "Love and serve each other."
Draw a picture that shows love.

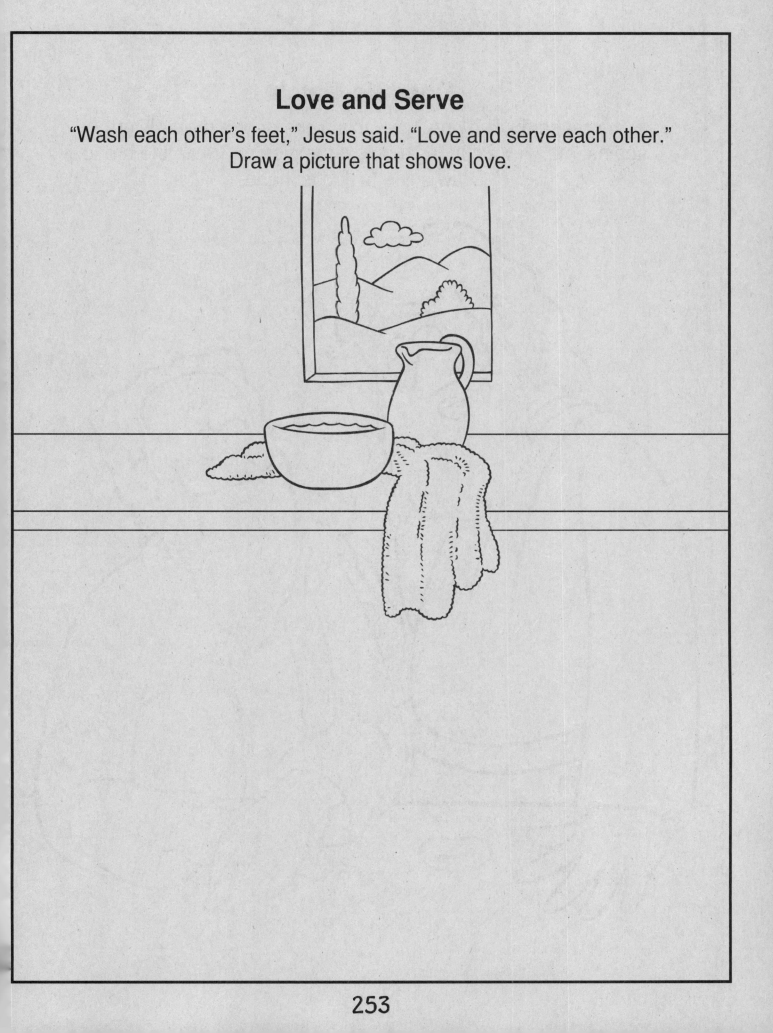

Does He Match

Jesus said, "The one I give this piece of bread to will turn against me." It was Judas. Look at the picture. Circle the bread. Draw a line to Judas' hand.

Does Not Belong

Jesus said, "Do what you must." Judas quickly left.
Put on X on who does not belong in the picture.

Is It Broken

Jesus picked up a loaf of bread and blessed it. He broke it into pieces.
Put an X on what is broken.

Jesus' Words

Jesus gave the bread to his disciples. "This bread is my body,"
Jesus told the disciples. "Every time you eat it, think of me."
Find and circle the words in the puzzle below.

BREAD **BLESSED** **BROKE**

BLOOD **BODY** **BELONG**

E V Y I N C P B

B R E A D B Z L

R K R E D E G E

O T B O J L P S

K B O D Y O P S

E L V F J N L E

B S Q I V G M D

What Next, Jesus?

Jesus took a cup of wine. "This is my blood. It is poured out to forgive the sins of many." Circle what comes next in the pattern.

Getting Ready

Jesus said, "I am going to heaven to prepare a home for you.
I will return." What kind of new home is Jesus preparing? Read the clues.
Circle the correct answer.

1. Jesus has to go away to prepare it.

2. The disciples cannot go there yet.

3. It will be wonderful.

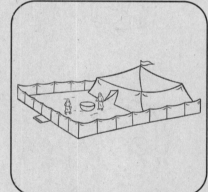

Happy or Sad

Jesus said, "At first, you will be very sad. Then you will be filled with joy."
Make an X on the sad faces. Circle the faces filled with joy.

Thirty in All

Judas asked the leaders how much money they would give him if he helped capture Jesus. "Thirty pieces of silver," the leaders said. Circle ten groups of three coins to make thirty.

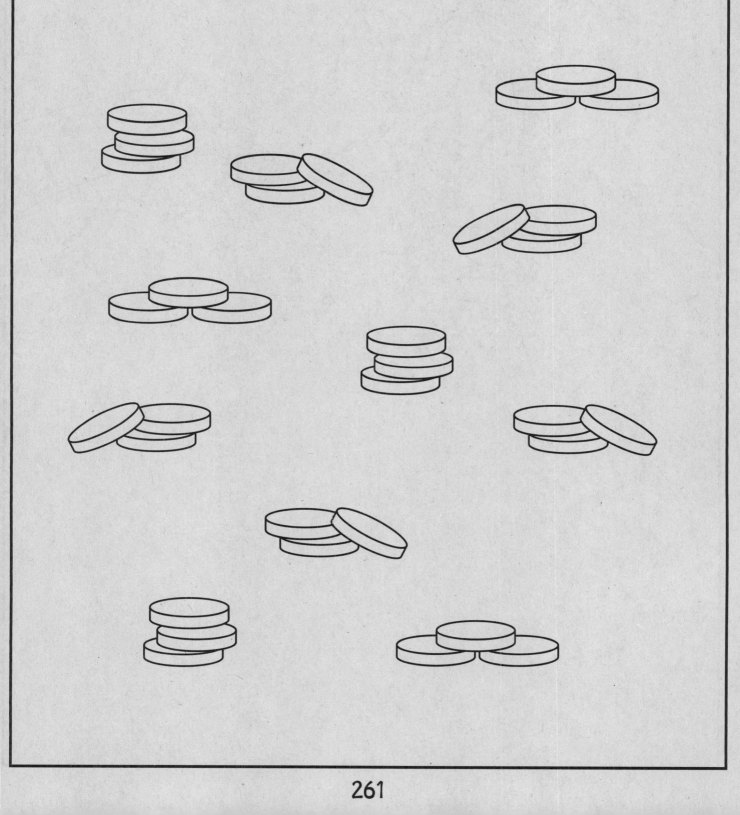

Pay Here

Jesus went to his favorite garden to pray. Draw a picture of a place to pray.

Give It All

Jesus prayed, "Father, I am ready to give my life to save the people from their sins." Jesus gave his life! Connect others to what they gave.

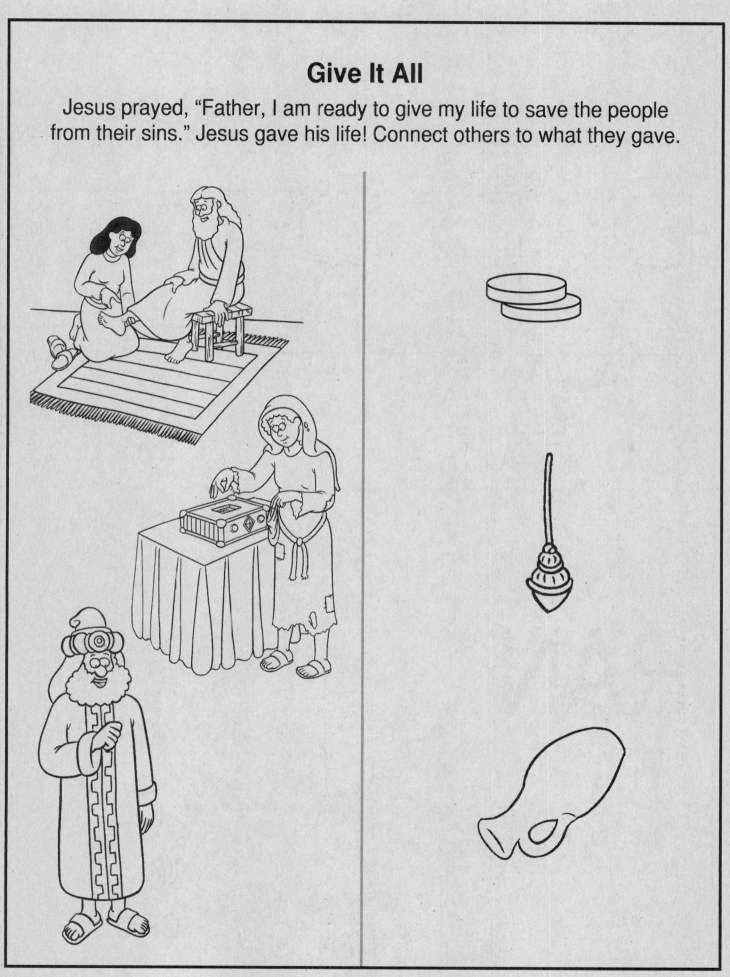

They Ran

The soldiers came to take Jesus. The disciples ran away.
Trace and write R. Trace RAN. Draw a line to the words that rhyme with RAN.

R R R R

RAN RAN

RAN

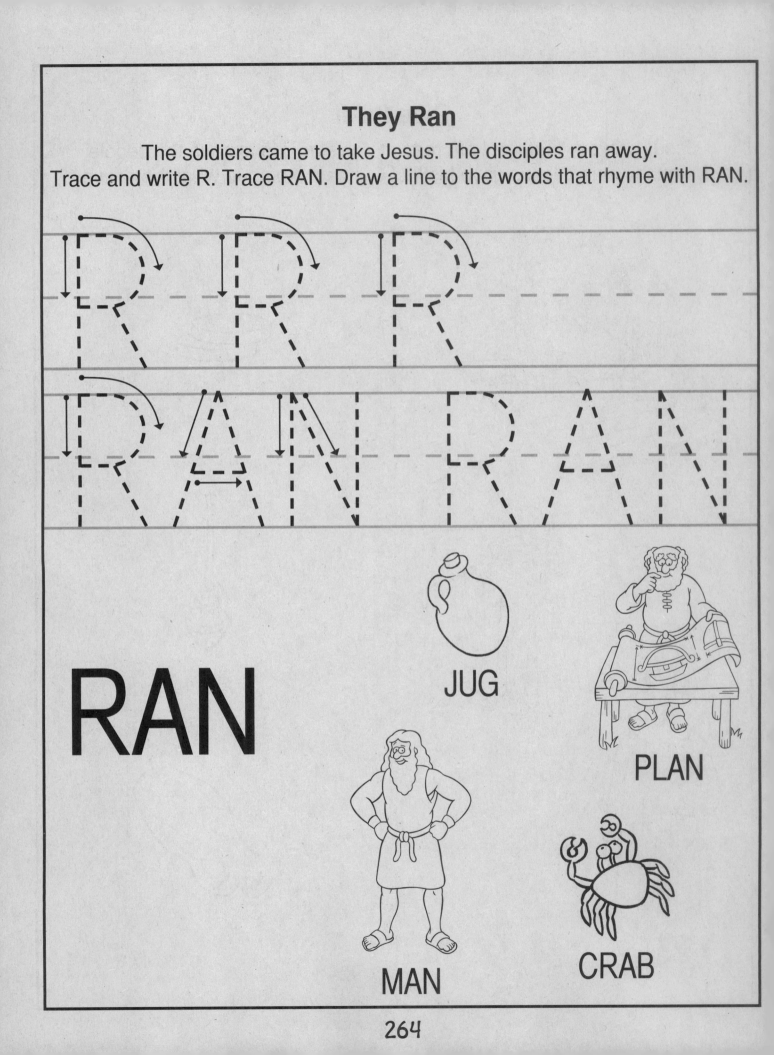

JUG

PLAN

MAN

CRAB

Not the Son?

The leaders said to Jesus, "No. You are not the Son of God."
Follow the directions below.

☐ Look at the three men. Draw an arrow (←) on the leader on the left.

☐ Draw an arrow (→) on the leader on the right.

☐ Make an X on the leader in between.

The leaders said,

"No. You are not the Son of God."
Could the leaders be right?

☐ Trace Not.

Jesus' Cross Is Heavy

The soldiers made Jesus carry a big wooden cross.
Trace the rectangles. Draw the cross Jesus had to carry.

Mary, Jesus' Mother

Jesus died on the cross. His mother Mary was with him.
Draw a line from Mary to her shadow.

1st, 2nd, 3rd

Jesus died on the cross. Write 1 below what happened first. Write 2 below what happened next. Write 3 below what happened last.

Yes, He IS

Everyone was sad. But they forgot! Jesus is the Son of God.
Trace and write I, S, IS!

Open or Closed

Some of Jesus' friends laid his body in a tomb. They closed it with a large round stone. Make an X on everything that is closed. Circle what is open.

Circle It

An angel came from heaven and pushed the stone away.
Trace the round stone. Trace the circles on the page.

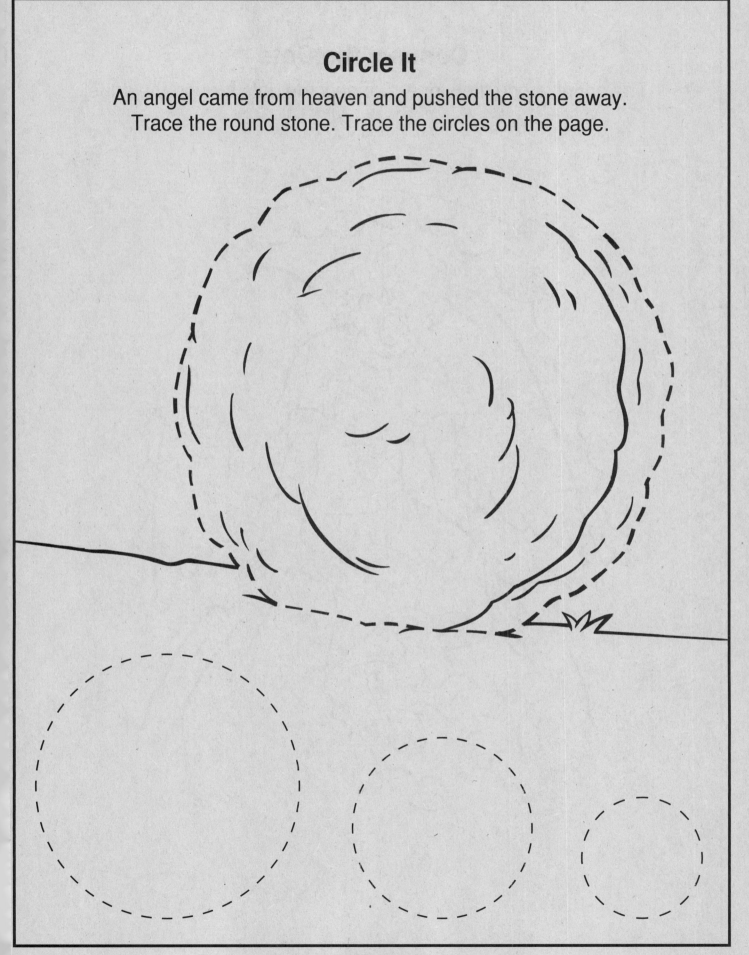

Connect the Dots

The angel sat on the stone. Connect the dots around the angel.

An Angel?

Jesus' mother Mary and her friends saw the angel. The angel said, "Do not be afraid." Who has seen an angel? Draw a line to connect the pictures to the angel.

Not Here!

The angel said, "Jesus is not here. He has risen!"
Circle who has risen.

Help with the Message

The women saw Jesus. Jesus said, "Go tell the others."
Run with Mary to tell the others!

Inside the Room

The disciples were afraid. They locked themselves in a small room.
Put an X on what is in.

Peace

Suddenly, Jesus appeared! He said, "Peace be with you."
Color the peaceful picture.

Between You and Me

Jesus stood between the disciples so they could touch his hands and feet. Circle the person between the others.

So Happy

The disciples were very, very happy to see Jesus again.
Circle the picture that shows why the disciples were happy.

Empty Nets

The disciples went fishing. They did not even catch one fish.
The net was empty. Make an X on the pictures that show empty.

Move Left to Right

Early the next morning, someone yelled from the shore,
"Cast your net to the right side of the boat."
Draw an arrow (→) to move the circled item from the left to the right.

Please Count

As soon as the disciples moved the net, the net was full of sea creatures!
Count the creatures in the net. Circle the answer.

I See Jesus

Peter knew the man on the shore was Jesus. Peter jumped into the water and swam to shore. Draw a man going to see Jesus.

How to Love

Jesus asked Peter, "Do you love me?"
Draw a picture that shows a way to love someone.

I DO!

Peter said, "You know I do." Trace and write I, DO. Draw a line to the words that rhyme with DO.

DO

CHEW

TWO

MOO

BURN

Caring is Important

Jesus said, "If you love me, take care of my people."
Draw a line to connect the people who care with Jesus.

Good News

It was time for Jesus to leave. Jesus told the disciples to tell everyone the good news. Tell the people on the left, on the right, beside, and between! Circle the person sharing the good news of Jesus. Make an X on the man beside him. Circle the girl between.

More Believers

Jesus told the disciples to make more disciples.
Draw more disciples. Give them names.

Over and Under

Jesus told the disciples to baptize the new disciples.
John baptized in the river Jordan. He helped the people go under the water. Draw an arrow (↓) pointing to under. Circle what is over the water.

Count the Commandments

Jesus told the disciples to teach the new disciples to obey his commandments. Count the commandments. Trace the number that tells how many.

1. GOD IS THE ONLY TRUE GOD.

2. NEVER MAKE IDOLS.

3. NEVER MISUSE THE LORD'S NAME.

4. REST ON THE SABBATH DAY, KEEP IT HOLY.

5. HONOR YOUR FATHER AND YOUR MOTHER.

6. DO NOT MURDER.

7. HUSBANDS AND WIVES MUST NOT COMMIT ADULTERY.

8. DO NOT STEAL.

9. DO NOT TELL LIES.

10. NEVER WANT WHAT BELONGS TO OTHERS.

10   12

Circle Around

Jesus said, "Don't ever forget. I will always be with you."
There is no beginning and no end to a circle. Trace the circles.

Take That Road

Jesus told the disciples, "Go to Jerusalem and wait there."
Draw a line to show the disciples the way to Jerusalem.

Opposites

It was time for Jesus to leave. He could not stay.
Leave and stay are opposites. Connect the opposites.

Don't Be Afraid

Jesus said, "Do not be afraid." Color the picture.

Up, Up, Up

Jesus went up towards heaven. Circle what is up.

All the Same

The angels said, "Jesus will return the same way you saw him go."
Color the picture that is the same as the first one.

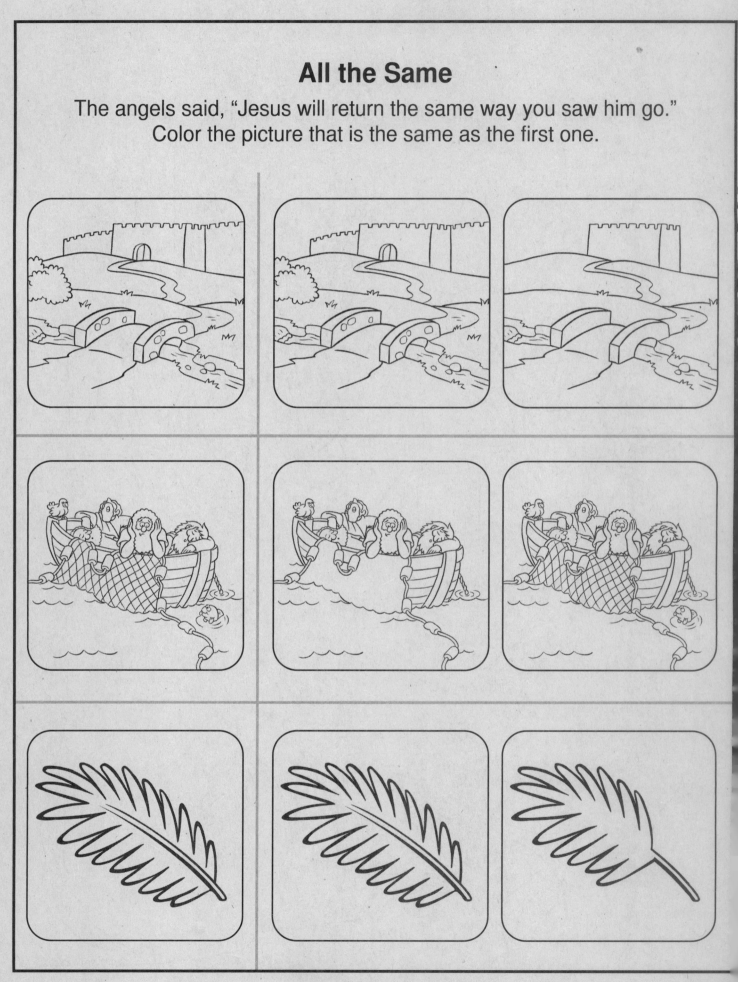

Is It Different?

People from many different countries came to Jerusalem.
They spoke many different languages. Circle the picture that is different.

Blowing Strong

The disciples were praying. A noise like a wind filled the room.
Circle where the wind is blowing.

Tongues of Fire

The Holy Spirit appeared as tongues of fire on each of the disciples.
Trace and write F. Color the flames on the disciples.

Hello to All People

The disciples started talking in many languages.
Find and circle the words that all mean hello in the puzzle below.

HOLA   **BONJOUR**   **HELLO**

SALAAM   **SHALOM**

```
B O N J O U R C
I B Z X E D L I
W S A K G B U R
T C A H E L L O
S D X L T B F R
V H O L A J K L
O N H R C A S W
B S H A L O M S
```

Many, Many

Peter told the crowd, "God sent Jesus to save everyone."
A crowd is many. Circle the pictures that show many.

I Am Sorry

Peter said, "Tell Jesus you are sorry for your sins and be baptized." Draw a picture of something for which you are sorry. It is for Jesus.

Dear Jesus,
    I am sorry. I love you.

Three Thousand!

On that day, the disciples baptized 3,000 people. Trace and write 3. Trace and write 0. Trace and write 3,000. Circle the group of three.

Next, Please!

The new believers learned about God and the pattern of God's plan.
Circle the picture that comes next.

Make Music

The new believers prayed together and sang songs to God!
Circle the pictures that help make music.

Sharing God's Love

The new believers ate meals together and shared everything.
Draw a line from those who shared to what they shared.

It Is Good News

Share the good news of Jesus.
Color a picture for the letter below. Cut it out and give it away.

Dear _____,

Jesus is the Good News!

More and More

God added more and more believers to the church every day.
Circle the group that shows more.

Jesus' Loving Words

The lame man could not walk. He was begging.
Circle the picture of what the lame man wanted.

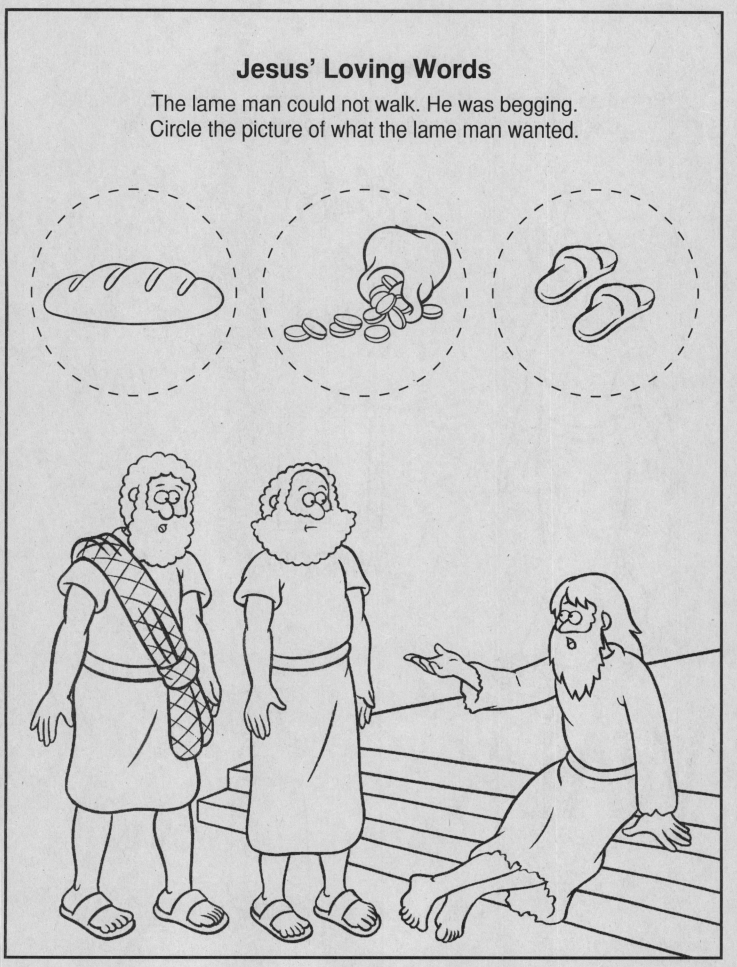

The W Sound

Peter had no money. He said, "In Jesus' name, stand up and walk."
Circle the words that begin with the same sound as walk.

CROWN

WAVE

WINDOW

HELMET

WALK

WOMAN

Leap, Leap, Leap

The man jumped up, leaping and praising God!
Circle the words that rhyme with leap.

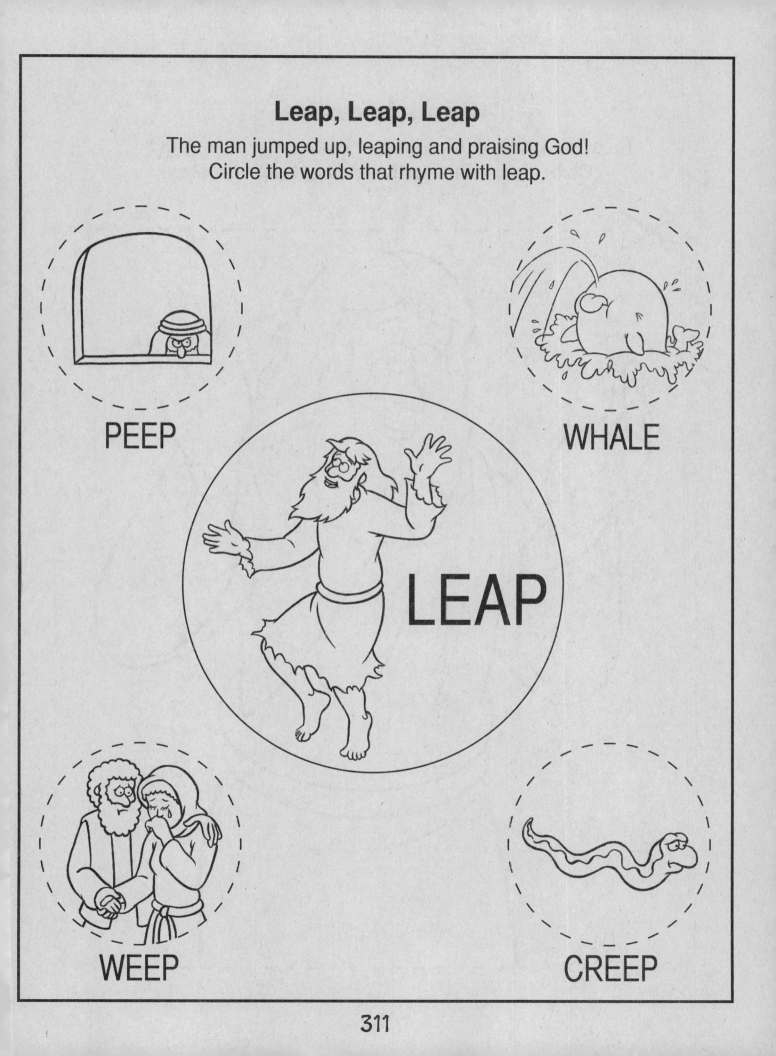

PEEP

WHALE

LEAP

WEEP

CREEP

Jesus Loves Me

Peter said, "We did not make the man walk. Jesus did it."
Color Jesus. Cut out the picture. Keep it nearby.

Saul Was Sad

Saul did not like the followers of Jesus.
Draw a square around the angry faces.

Jesus Is the Light

When Saul was walking, a bright light flashed around him.
A voice said, "I am Jesus." Trace I AM JESUS. Color the bright light.

I

AM

JESUS

Jesus, Help Me See

Saul could not see. Trace the ovals. Color the pictures over with black.

See God's Love

Ananias laid his hands on Saul and said, "Jesus sent me to you. You may see again." Trace the pictures of what Saul can see again. Color the pictures.

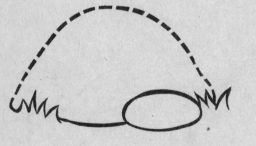

You Are Paul

God changed Saul's name to Paul. Circle PAUL.

SAUL

PAUL

PAUL

SAUL

SAUL

SAUL

PAUL

SAUL

PAUL

SAUL

Go Far and Wide

Paul traveled far and wide. Trace the wide rectangles.

A New Name

The new believers were called Christians. They followed Jesus Christ.
Draw a line from the picture to the name it is called.

CAT

DOG

MAN

GIRL

BOY

In ABC Order

Paul started many new churches. The believers met together.
Follow the letters in A-B-C order to finish the church building.
Color the church building.

Following God's Way

Paul walked many miles. Sometimes he took a boat across the seas.
Connect the dots to see some of the Paul's travels.

It Is All Good News!

Paul told everyone about Jesus' love for them. Color the picture.

God Protects

Some people did not like Paul and his friend, Silas, preaching about Jesus. One day they were thrown in prison. Paul and Silas knew God would take care of them.
Circle the pictures of who God took care of in prison.

Before or After

God sent an earthquake. The doors flew open! The chains fell off!
Circle 1 next to the picture of before the earthquake.
Circle 2 next to the picture of after the earthquake.

It Was a Puzzle

The guard thought everyone had escaped! Paul told the guard, "We are still here." Draw a line to connect the piece of the picture that makes the picture complete.

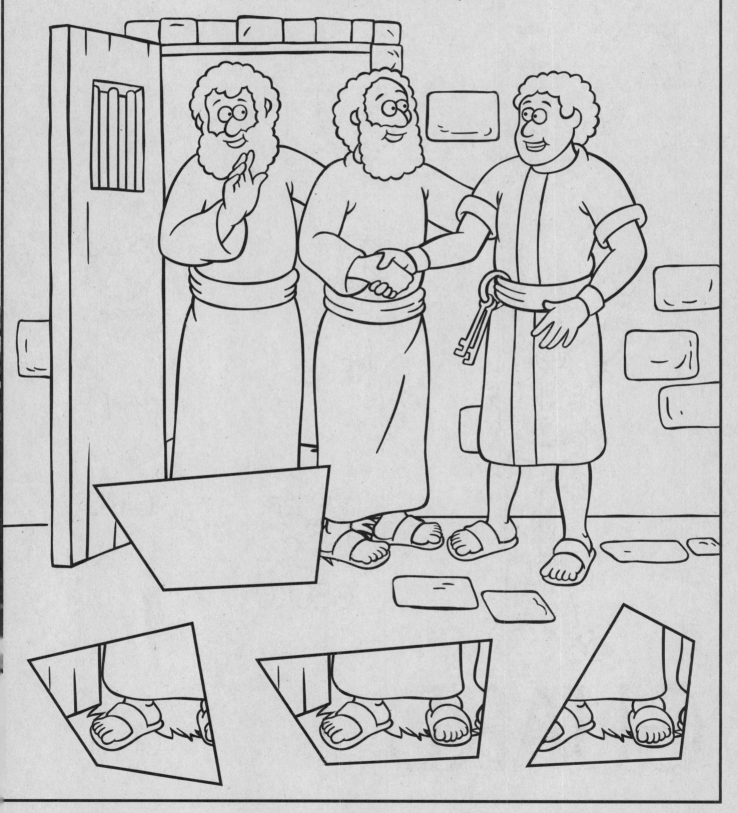

The G Sound

The guard and his family learned about Jesus and decided to follow him. Trace and write G. Circle the pictures that have the same beginning sound of G.

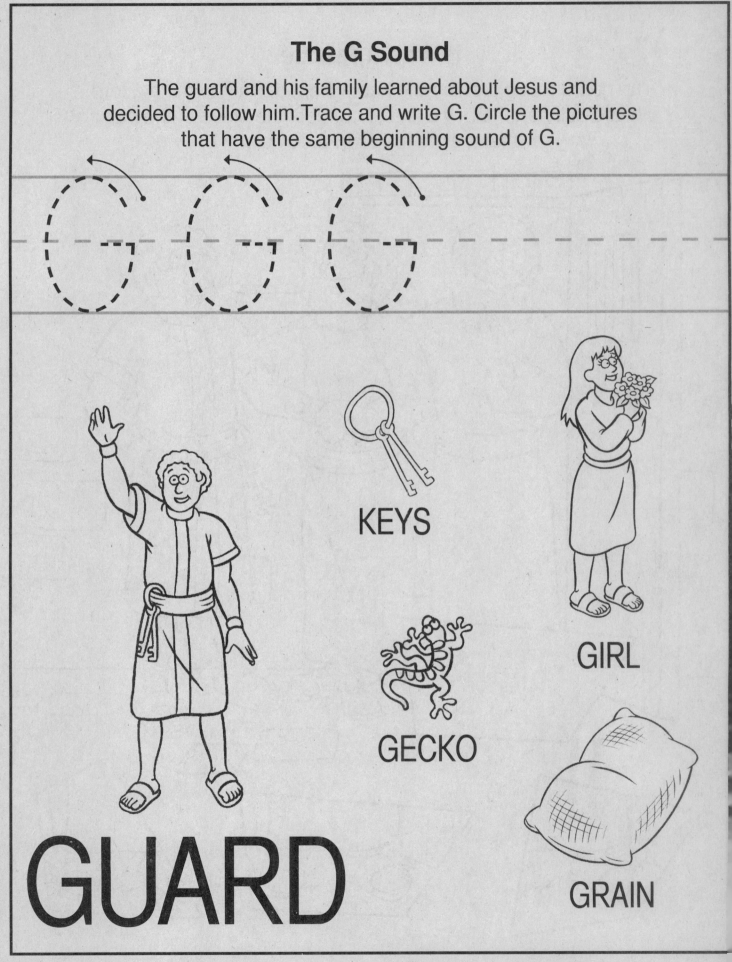

KEYS

GIRL

GECKO

GRAIN

GUARD

Follow the Trail

Many years later, the disciple John saw Jesus in a vision.
Jesus said, "Write a book about what I will show you."
John's book is in the Bible. Follow the Bible story trail to connect the dots.

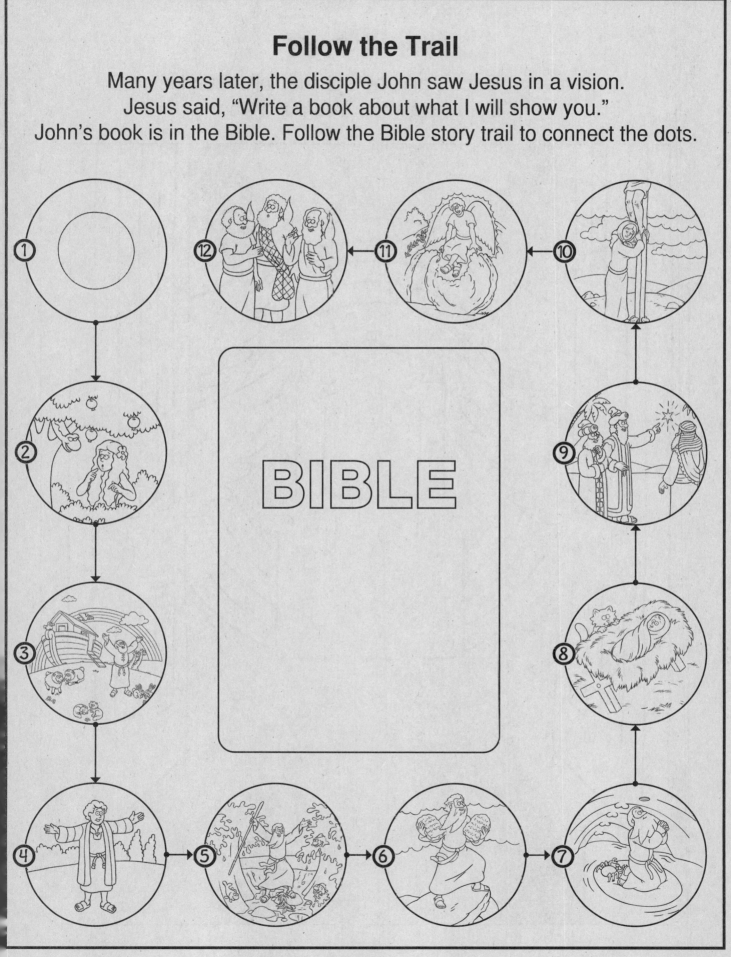

It Is All Good

John saw God. A rainbow sparkled all around him.
Color the rainbow all around God.

A New Heaven and Earth

John saw a new heaven and a new earth.
Color the new heaven and new earth.

Sadness Is Not Here

In the new heaven and new earth, there will be no death, sadness, crying, or pain. Make an X on what does not belong in the new heaven and new earth.

Find Jesus

Jesus promised, "I am coming back soon." Connect the dots.

Match The Beginner's Bible® Characters

Children love to play games. Memory games such as this game, similar to Concentration, will help your child recognize and remember the names of some well-known Bible figures.

1. Have your child color the pictures of the Bible characters. Suggest they color the two matching images the same to make the game a little easier.

2. Have your child trace the name of the character to help them remember the names.

3. Using child-safe scissors have your child cut apart the pictures, following the heavy, dashed line so that each picture is a rectangle. (Or you can do the cutting yourself.)

4. Shuffle the pictures and help your child arrange them, face down on a tabletop or the floor.

5. Begin the matching game by explaining that the child needs to find two matching pictures and be able to say that Bible character's name. He may flip two pictures over at a time. If there is not a match, or if the child says the wrong name, the pictures get flipped back over and the play begins again.

6. If the child gets a match, he takes the pictures and may flip two more.

7. Continue the game until all 16 matches have been made.

Another fun way to use these cards is to shuffle the pictures and have the child choose one character. Have the child say the character's name and give one or more facts about the life or Bible story that centers on that character. If they are correct, the child keeps the picture and may choose another.

ADAM

ADAM

EVE

EVE

NOAH

NOAH

ANGEL

ANGEL

DANIEL AND THE LION

DANIEL AND THE LION

JONAH

JONAH

DAVID

DAVID

GOLIATH

GOLIATH

SAMSON

SAMSON

MOSES

MOSES

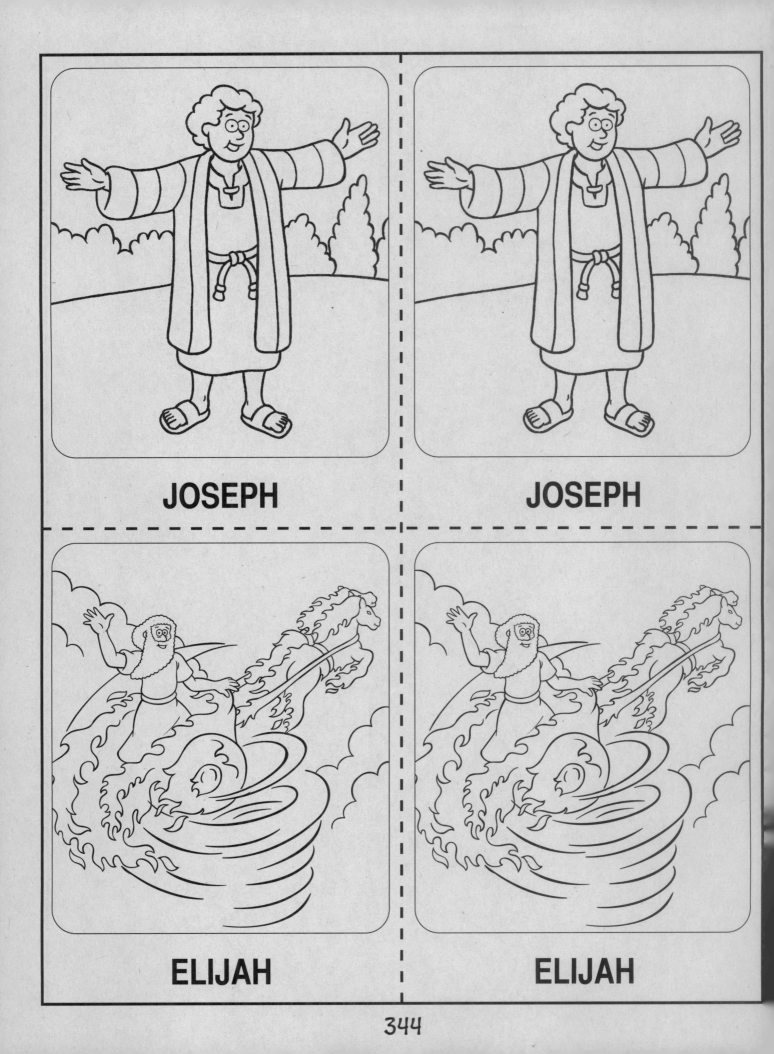

JOSEPH

JOSEPH

ELIJAH

ELIJAH

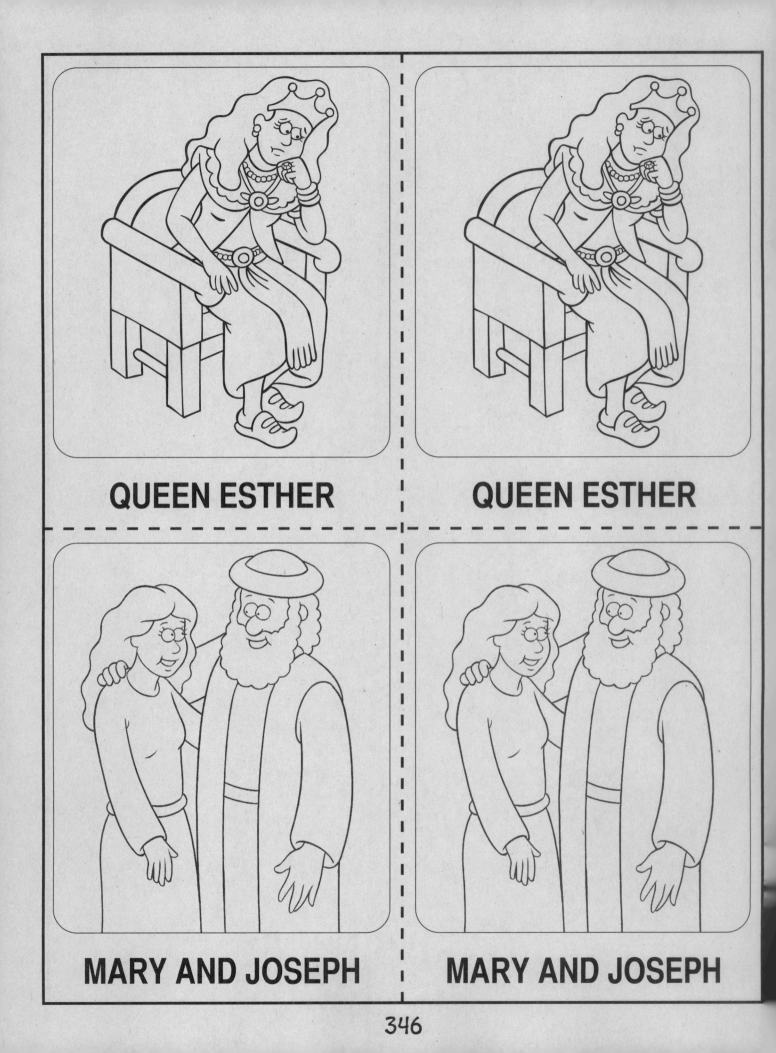

QUEEN ESTHER

QUEEN ESTHER

MARY AND JOSEPH

MARY AND JOSEPH

BABY JESUS

BABY JESUS

JESUS

JESUS

The Beginner's Bible® Number Cards

The following are a great resource to have for your young learner. This set of Number Cards can be colored, cut, and used to practice number recognition, counting 1–20, and putting items in number-order.

More things to do:

1. Say the number and the item on the card as your practice (ex. 1 ark).

2. Have your child trace over the numbers with a finger if they need practice with writing their numbers.

3. Shuffle the cards and place them face up on a tabletop. Help your child to arrange the cards in number order. As skill and knowledge progress you could challenge your child to just count or place the even- or odd-numbered cards.

4. Look through The Beginner's Bible® and count other examples of 1–20 images, or go beyond 20 and find 21 flowers, 22 trees, 23 jugs, and so on.

The Beginner's Bible® Puzzlers

Putting simple puzzles together is always fun.

Have your child color the following pictures as coloring pages. Then cut along the dotted lines, making the pictures into fun puzzles!

Talk about the Bible character and/or story in each puzzle as you put it together. Store the individual puzzles in small, zip-close bags for convenience and continued fun.

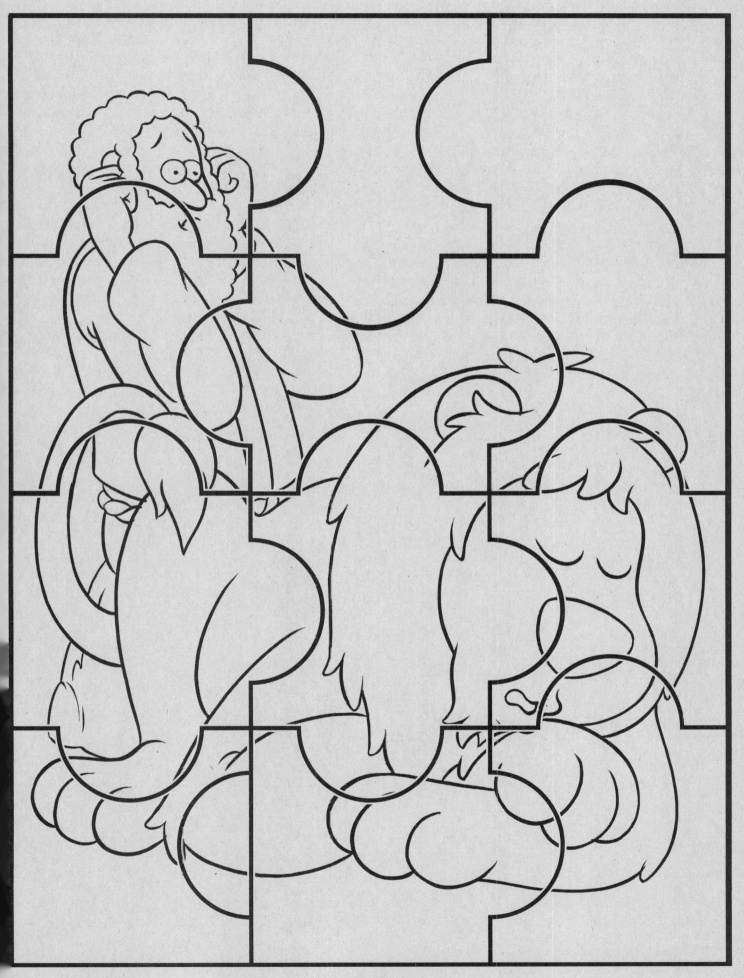

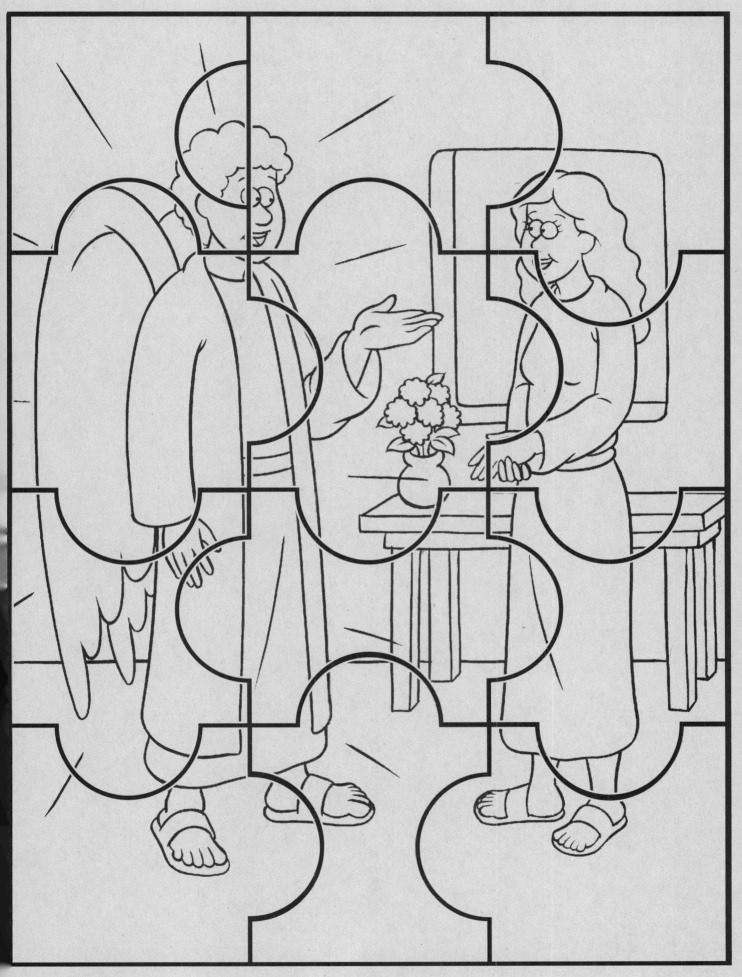

More The Beginner's Bible® Activity Pages

The following is a collection of assorted activity pages that can be done anytime. Use them as a family activity, a quiet-time task for little ones before bed, or even make several photocopies and use as a group activity with friends or brothers and sisters.

A Love Letter
Decorate this love letter to Jesus. Make it colorful and bright.

Dear God

Color this letter to God. Trace the letters. Sign your name.

Dear God,

I love you with all my heart.

I am your child.

Please help me every day!

Love,

_____

Finish the Picture

Finish this picture. Add trees, flowers, animals, and more.

Fill in the Blanks

Fill in the blanks. Use your best writing.

I _____ you, God.

You made the _____

and the _____.

My favorite part of creation is _____.

I promise to take care of _____.

Thank you,

_____

Which Are the Same?

See the birds. Three are the same. Color the birds that are exactly the same. Put an X on the two birds that are different.

A-Mazing!
Help Jesus find his friends.

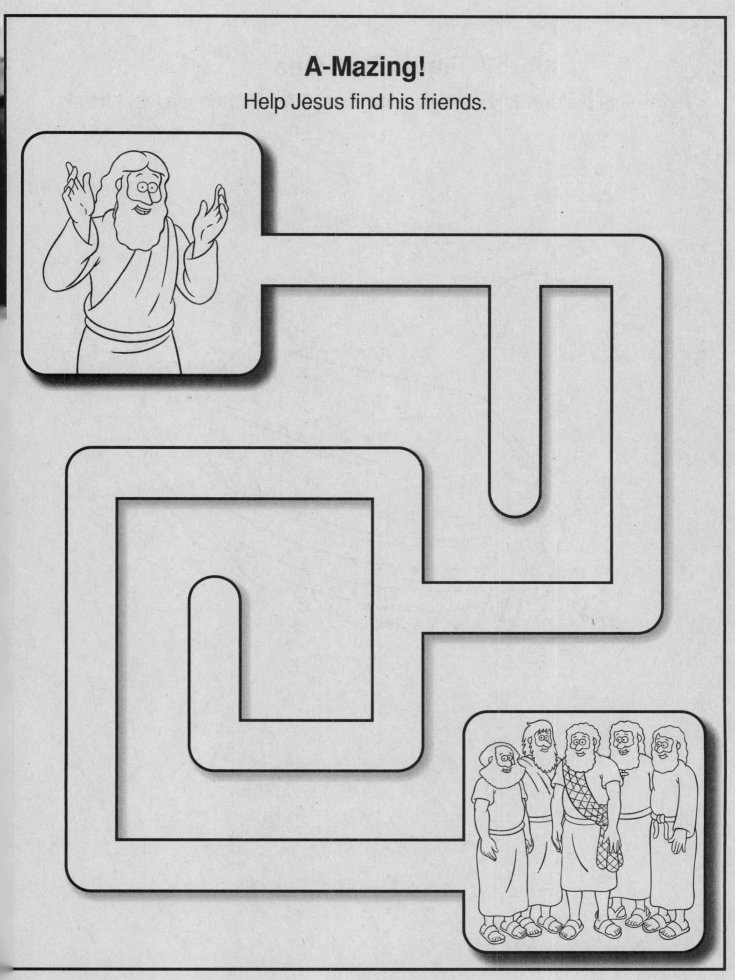

Finish This One

Finish this picture. Is it calm or is it stormy? Add water, waves, and sky.

Yes, He Does

Jesus loves you. Color this balloon.
Cut it out and hang it on your bedroom door.

JESUS LOVES ME!

Count How Many

Count how many monkeys. Write the number.
Count how many lizards. Write the number.

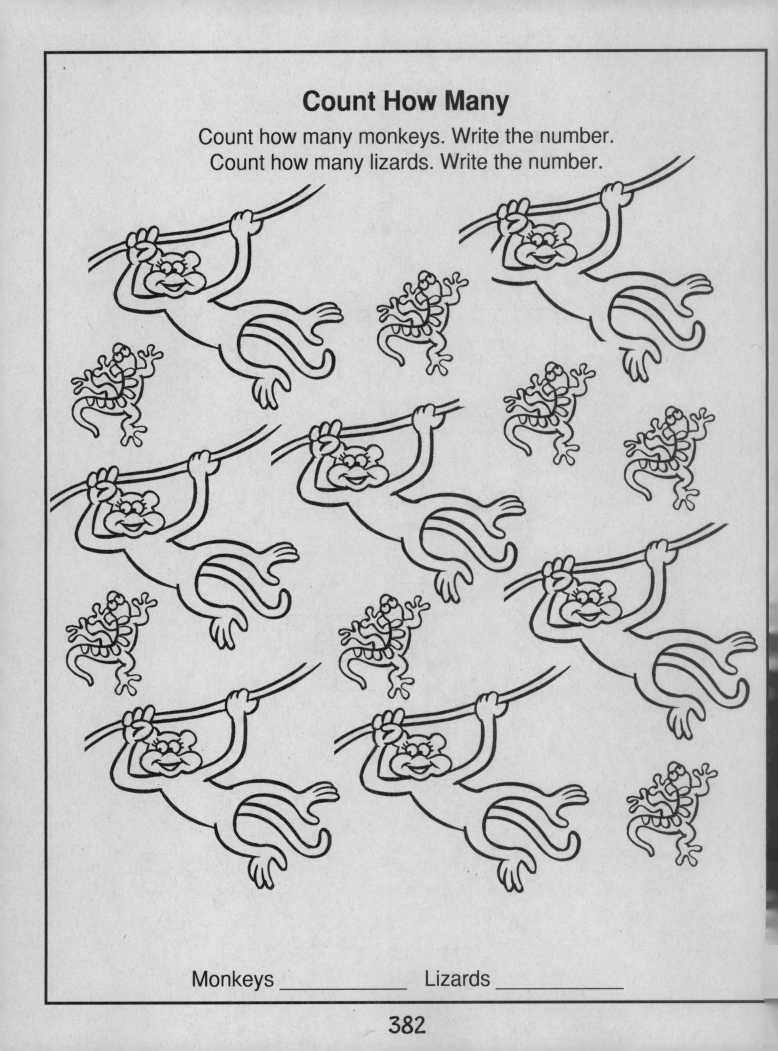

Monkeys _____   Lizards _____

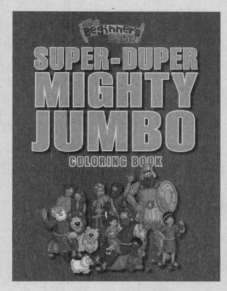

The Beginner's Bible

Building foundations of faith with children for over 30 years!

9780310750130
$18.99 / Hardcover

The Beginner's Bible® has been a favorite with young children and their parents since its release in 1989 with over 25 million products sold. While several updates have been made since its early days, *The Beginner's Bible®* will continue to build a foundation of faith in little ones for many more years to come.

Full of faith and fun, *The Beginner's Bible®* is a wonderful gift for any child. The easy-to-read text and bright, full-color illustrations on every page make it a perfect way to introduce young children to the stories and characters of the Bible. With new vibrant three-dimensional art and compelling text, more than 90 Bible stories come to life. Kids ages 6 and under will enjoy the fun illustrations of Noah helping the elephant onto the ark, Jonah praying inside the fish, and more, as they discover *The Beginner's Bible®* just like millions of children before. *The Beginner's Bible®* was named the 2006 Retailers Choice Award winner in Children's Nonfiction.

More products from *The Beginner's Bible®* to discover:

The Beginner's Bible
Activity Book
9780310759799

The Beginner's Bible
Coloring Book
9780310759553

The Beginner's Bible
Learn Your Letters
9780310770244

The Beginner's Bible
Learn Your Numbers
9780310770497

The Beginner's Bible
Preschool Workbook
9780310751670

The Beginner's Bible
Preschool Math Workbook
9780310138952

The Beginner's Bible
All Aboard Noah's Ark
9780310768678

The Beginner's Bible
Read Through the Bible
9780310752806